Contents

THE **SPONTANEOUS** **SPREAD** OF **HOME-DISCIPLESHIP** **CHRISTIANITY**

HENRY REYENGA JR.

HOME DISCIPLESHIP PRESS

To Rich and Helen DeVos,
Marty and Ruth Ozinga,
Ron and Cheri Parr,
and to my family

Introduction

IT WAS September 1993, and I was shooting baskets with my 7-year-old son in the driveway of our home in Colorado Springs. My neighbor, a retired Air Force enlisted man, walked over to join us. He had a speech impediment, so he wasn't often talkative, but that day he began to share with me about his involvement in Amway, a multilevel-marketing business. He wanted me to try it as well. He did not try to impress me with facts and figures; he did not talk to me about the high quality of the products; he simply shared with me a dream. I asked him why he was doing this business, and he told me of his dream to get out of debt and provide for his family. He told me that he was just barely making it—but his business had given him hope. He had found faith in free enterprise.

I was impressed. I saw an ordinary guy with a clear dream. He had a tool to make that dream happen; his clear and reproducible business model was one anybody could follow. His urgency to help me start my own business trumped his fears and limitations. His dream was real to him, and he wasn't going to be easily discouraged.

I told my neighbor I wasn't interested in seeing the plan, but our conversation stuck in my mind anyway. This man made me think about Christianity. What if Christians had such urgency to share their walks with God? What if Christians were more aware of the spiritual dreams that motivate and drive them? What if Christians had the tools to share their dream with their neighbors and coworkers? This man made me dream of a Christianity that would spontaneously spread from house to house, from person to person. I realized that, as a lifelong church planter, my usual models and plans had relied little on this kind of natural enthusiasm. I was ready for a change.

Since graduating from Calvin Seminary in 1987, I had attended more than thirty church-growth seminars, and I was trying to be like the mega-church pastors. I had just left one church plant and was about to begin another one. Right after graduation, I was involved in planting a church that drew from the best of the American church-growth movement. Our church grew to several hundred in five years from 1988-1993. We were introducing dramas, transitioning the music to mesh better with the sounds of contemporary culture, and focusing our messages on life application. In those days, we repeated slogans like "find a need and fill it" and "we're a seeker-driven church" over and over. Our church constantly looked to establish new and more meaningful programs that accurately fit people's life situations. I enjoyed the work: the networking, the dramas, the music, the messages. I enjoyed the crowds and the answered prayers.

However, I was ready for a change because I realized that planting a church was becoming too involved. I was ready for a change because I realized that the church-growth paradigm in America pushed every planter to define success as the creation of a mega-church. This required extraordinary leaders. It required a lot of money and staff. I began to realize that another model had to be found that would contribute to the spontaneous spread of Christianity. The seeds of home-discipleship Christianity were planted.

I was familiar with the mega-church model. Mega-churches are very effective at getting people "in the front door." The entertaining worship and relevant topics, along with active promotion and word of mouth, bring people inside. The goal is then to disciple them though small groups and programs. This model needs a large critical mass and large amounts of staff and money for it to be effective. This model sets the bar at becoming a mega-church. So most leaders who want to grow their churches go to seminars put on by mega-church leaders, like Bill Hybels from Willow Creek Community Church or Rick Warren from Saddleback Community Church.

Is there anything lacking with that? At one level the answer is no. The Holy Spirit changes lives any time God is worshipped and the Word is preached, whether at a worship service or in a programmatic small-group setting. And God has always and will always use the corporate body, the church, as one of the key instruments to reach people.

At another level, I can think of one thing lacking in the mega-church model. This model requires very exceptional leadership skills. We have seen in America some exceptional preachers and pastors with name recognition across the entire country. God has used these extraordinary leaders to set the pace for the church-growth movement even as it spreads to other countries. What is lacking in this model? If our church-growth operating system is too dependent and really works best when exceptionally gifted leaders are required, the mission of the church-growth movement will be ultimately handicapped. What made America fill with over 400,000 churches was not the exceptionally gifted leaders with mega-church qualities. It was the ordinary leaders. It happened through churches of 100, of 200, of 500. As for mega-churches, they will always be around, but our model for expanding the Christian movement had better be something more ordinary.

The church began with twelve ordinary men whose only qualification was that they had been with Jesus. The disciples were mainly lowly fishermen. Early in the spreading of the new church, Peter and John were dragged before the big-shot religious leaders. These men saw whom Jesus had picked as leaders in spreading his new teachings. Luke wrote in Acts:

> When they saw the courage of Peter and John and realized that they were unschooled, ordinary men, they were astonished and they took note that these men had been with Jesus. (Acts 4:13)

What impressed me about my neighbor, this Amway distributor, was how ordinary he really was. He was an enlisted man. He had an ordinary life. In his association with Amway, he received a real dream. He told me how he used the products, but he wasn't simply pushing detergent and potato chips. He had a message of free enterprise. He described how his life had changed and he wanted to share this all with me. Wow! Amway had figured out how to help an ordinary guy do amazing feats. If only the ordinary Christian would have such a transforming walk with God and would be willing to share it so freely.

"Will You Be My Mentor?"

After this meeting with my neighbor, I came to the conclusion that I needed one of the founders of Amway Corporation to mentor me. I figured that I could learn something that would have powerful application for the work of the church. I sent a fax to the Amway headquarters, attention Mr. Rich DeVos. I told him in the fax that his work in establishing Amway and figuring out how to help ordinary people start and share businesses was very important. Within 24 hours, Rich DeVos called me and agreed to be my mentor. He gave me his home phone numbers. He even gave me his cell numbers. I concluded that God had a great purpose and I was looking forward to finding out how this new relationship was going to bear fruit.

Together with fellow church planter Steve Elzinga, who had a similar passion to see the spontaneous spread of Christianity everywhere, I began meeting regularly with Rich DeVos. I even joined Amway in order to understand how this business model reproduced. In fact, the wife of Dr. Carl George, Grace, sponsored me. Within a short time, I sponsored many distributors. But my ultimate goal was to learn the secrets of effectively reproducing the walk and culture of Christianity.

I found out that multilevel marketing was a business model based on the family tree. Amway was "generations" of business owners. A sponsor was a father/mother, so to speak, and a new business owner a son/daughter. The goal was to have many children, grandchildren, great-grandchildren, great-great-grandchildren, and so on. This is very understandable and simple. But it takes leadership intentionality and a clear focus of what you are called to reproduce.

Rich DeVos identified several foundations to the success of sponsoring millions of Amway distributors, many bases that we found to have direct connection to the Bible's way of spreading the movement of Christianity. God used Mr. DeVos to help me see the walk and spread of Christianity in a deeper way than I had known. Someone may question why a discussion of network marketing really applies to the spontaneous spread of Christianity. I believe that the reason Amway is so successful is that it empowered people to be active participants in getting their dreams—to be players rather than spectators in the game of business. Amway gives its business owners a reproducible business pattern that is supported by sponsors, recognition, business leaders, small groups, and large groups. Amway distributors are carried along by a culture of those who are like-minded in their free-enterprise goals. The genius of Amway is that it helps ordinary people to be something they never dreamed they were capable of being.

Home-discipleship Christianity, as it has developed over the years, has begun to have a similar effect on the lives of ordinary Christians. It has mobilized Christians to do more for God than they ever thought they could. People who thought they could never talk about their faith or disciple someone in a relationship with God are finding that it's possible. This paradigm does not rely on talented, articulate speakers to motivate people to spend time with God, but on mentoring relationships wherein people spend time with God together, walking alongside each other. It identifies simple day-in, day-out habits of walking with God that neighbors can do with neighbors, parents can do with children, workers can do with coworkers. Home-discipleship Christianity encourages people to be players, not spectators, in their spiritual dreams. It gives people a plan for connecting to God that can be reproduced in the lives of anyone they meet. It is supported by a network of like-minded Christians who are reinforcing the same habits in their families and churches, who help to overcome obstacles and setbacks together. By God's grace, the home-discipleship movement is seeing a spontaneous spread. People are simply eager to share the effects of a vital relationship with God, and they have a framework with which to pass it on.

If you want to discover the principles behind home-discipleship Christianity, keep reading. If you want to discover how your church can benefit from a common goal of home discipleship, keep reading. If you want to see a change in yourself or your family because your spiritual life has become dry and tired, keep reading. If you want to find the courage to share your walk with God, maybe for the first time, then keep reading. It is my hope and dream that God will use this book to make your faith stronger, more alive, more contagious. I hope that you will find the motivation and the tools to experience a Christian life that spreads spontaneously.

Chapter 1

Life in a Home-Discipleship Church

WHEN YOU walk through the doors of our home-discipleship church, you will probably notice a few things different from your typical American church. To start with, there are young children sitting in the congregation. They have not been shuttled off to Sunday school, separated from their parents and older siblings. Children learn and worship in the context of their family. You might next notice that during the singing of hymns, the congregation sings in four-part harmony. During the preaching, you might notice that most people are paying attention, even children. Later you will discover that each family had already read the portion of Scripture covered by the sermon, and were supplementing their own discussions and understanding of the passage. You might also see the congregation recite a Bible passage together from memory, in a strong and unified voice. It will be hard to miss that the families in our church are players, not spectators, in a walk with God.

Our church is not "seeker sensitive" in the traditional sense of the phrase, which indicates eliminating anything that might make the newcomer uncomfortable or confused. But when you read the above paragraph, did you find your heart leap at any point? Did you feel a longing stirred within you to see a portion of that happen in your own church or your own family? Anyone who is truly seeking after God knows that the climb is steep and the road rocky but that the journey is worth it. Those who seek are not after the bare-minimal requirements but aspire to the rich full life of a diligent pursuit of God.

At a home-discipleship church, the structure of the church exists to support reading and studying the Bible, praying, singing, and memorizing Scripture in a person's home life. The Sunday service is a celebration, the culmination of the work put into a walk with God in the context of one's home and family throughout the week. It is a thanksgiving gift to God; we are not there primarily to receive. Unlike churches I've pastored in the past, the burden and attention is not all on me as the pastor. Every family that is successful in its home-discipleship walk is truly a leader; in fact, several groups of families have gone on to reproduce their walk with others and plant daughter churches as their intentionality together has grown.

Each home-discipleship church will grow differently and has its own story to tell; that it part of what it means to spread spontaneously. But let me further paint a picture of the life of a home-discipleship church by telling the genesis of the first one, Family of Faith Church, which began in May of 2000.

It began with a monthly hymn sing—just an informal gathering of people who missed the old hymns and who were looking to teach them to our children. We also desired encouragement in reading the Bible and praying with our children on a regular basis. By inviting several friends and friends of friends, we gathered about twenty-five people in my barn in Beecher, Illinois, and had a potluck. We sang a few old hymns together, ate food, and then made a few homework assignments: We committed to learn "He Leadeth Me" for the hymn of the month. We committed to memorize a Bible passage and make time for family devotions in our homes. We explained that doing home discipleship was very simple but not necessarily easy. We would meet the next month to recite the Bible memory passages together.

Finding at least fifteen minutes a day to read the Bible as a family, memorize Scripture, and sing the hymn of the month was challenging for each family. Every family ran up against some brick walls. I remember one that my family faced around that time: A month before the group hymn sing started, we picked a hymn as a family: "I Need Thee Every Hour." One of my children would not sing. I said: We are going to sing verse one until everyone sings. This one child did not sing until we had done the first verse fifteen times. Under sibling pressure, this child finally gave in and sang. Now this child loves singing with the family. All the families faced similar types of walls in claiming fifteen to thirty minutes of home discipleship each day, but they also had made a commitment to show up the next month and didn't want to be the only family who had made no progress. Hard as it was, everyone kept at it.

In June of 2000, we met for a hymn sing again. This time the number of attendees doubled. Three new families had been invited to see families recite Scripture and support their friends in home discipleship. The June event was moving. Some of the fathers who had never before recited Scripture with their family rose to the occasion. Many of us felt emotionally touched by what we saw: recitations of Scriptures and enthusiastic singing of hymns, even by people who thought they disliked hymns. We saw families who never memorized anything actually succeed in memorizing. At times, many of us had goose bumps from the experience.

The hymn sing represented the power of encouragement—of accountability, of iron sharpening iron. Many families had tried and failed in attempting some kind of home discipleship in the past. Many families had never even encountered home discipleship, and were trying something new for the first time. But together, by recognizing and celebrating families who were succeeding, we were creating a culture where home discipleship was achievable.

It was fascinating to evaluate the importance of encouragement. The apostle Paul wrote in Philippians 3:17:

> Join with others in following my example, brothers, and take note of those who live according to the pattern we gave you.

As a group we "took note" of families who desired to practice home discipleship for fifteen minutes a day. We found that public recognition was a positive and fun form of accountability that the family could use to read the Bible, memorize Scriptures, and sing together. At first, people seemed to be highly motivated by the public recognition; soon they were motivated instead by the tangible change they saw in their family when the Word of God was a central daily feature in their home. We noticed that fathers were really starting to get into it. Many times, fathers would give spontaneous testimonies to what God was doing in their personal lives and in the lives of their families.

As the fall of 2000 played itself out, the hymn sing almost doubled again. At that time, about 80 people were gathering in my barn to recite Scripture and sing hymns on the first Saturday of the month. We had done no advertising; families were just inviting other families who they knew had a similar interest in discipleship within the home. One of the friends we invited was a buddy of mine from seminary, Rev. David Feddes. He and his family attended the first meeting in May, and as the gatherings grew in size and in their effect on people, Dave and I came together with our wives to pray about transitioning our meetings into a full-fledged home-discipleship church. We each had a desire to nurture our families in the context of a group devoted to home discipleship. Dave and I had a long discussion about our views on most ministry topics. We both had full-time ministry jobs but felt God was leading us to partner in planting Family of Faith Church.

We set the date for the first worship to be the first Sunday of January 2001. Along with some lay families that had joined the effort right away, we insulated my metal barn and put a furnace in it for heating. We bought a small sound system. We invited everyone from the hymn sings, but we knew that if the novelty of home discipleship had worn off, or if the commitment was just too high, this would be an ideal time for people to bow out. We had no idea if people would want to come to a home-discipleship church. By the third Sunday, though, we were cramming in more than 125 people in a space for one hundred. Our church was three weeks old, and we already had to find a new place to meet.

We started leasing a nearby church building, a much larger space that could accommodate growth. Within a year and a half, the church had expanded to the point that it bought the building and property. The vision of home discipleship was spontaneously spreading. More and more families attended as people shared with friends and neighbors about what was happening in their families. Home discipleship was making a difference.

In 2004, we needed to do a building expansion to double the size of our sanctuary. We have planted daughter churches and impacted the broader kingdom of God with the development of our Christian Leaders training organization. We are continually amazed by what God is doing through the small seed he planted in that first hymn sing. Our church did not advertise; we did not do a telemarketing effort; we did not have a grand opening service. We are simply reaching individuals, couples, and families who believe that if their faith walk within the home wins, then the church will win, too.

*   *   *

A Deeper Look

Brian and Kristi have made a profound ministry out of hospitality at our church. If you visit Family of Faith, it is likely that the
Brian and Kristi will invite you to their home within a couple of
weeks. Their family offers encouragement and hospitality that
even goes beyond a Sunday dinner. If someone is moving, I have
seen Kristi just show up with the cleaning supplies. Their children have also contributed to making new families feel at home.
Brian has served as an elder for quite a while and has a passion
for making the home-discipleship vision a welcoming force at
Family of Faith Church.

Many churches have welcoming teams and hospitality coor-
dinators, but what's unique about hospitality at Family of Faith
is that we don't invite you to dinner only for social conversation.
It's that our homes are the real center of activity in the church,
and we want to connect you with them. The opportunity to hang
around other families that are serious about practicing their
faith in their home is crucial. This time of fellowship does a lot
to show that home discipleship is about real lives and real families. When a new family experiences doing devotions and
observes the Scripture memory of the host family, it gives the
visiting family a hope of being able to do likewise.

A home-discipleship family meeting involves four primary elements: reading the Scripture, prayer, Bible memorization, and
singing. We provide a family journal in which people can write
down their prayers—not just a list of requests but also confessions, praise, and thanks to God. We also provide a Bible-reading schedule that assigns a passage of Scripture to study each
day, and the entire church follows the same schedule. On
Sunday, the pastor will preach about one of the readings in
order to deepen what discussions and thoughts people have
already attached to the Bible passage. We also ask families to

work at memorizing a portion of the Bible each month, spending five minutes each day reciting it. At the end of the month's time, families receive the platform to recite the passage in front of the whole church. This is also our "hymn sing" time where we sing together the hymn of the month that families have spent each day singing together and learning to memorize.

Few other churches ask their congregations to prepare in advance for corporate worship, assuming that most people don't like to sing. What we have found is that people enjoy singing once they understand the style of the traditional hymns, which have four separate parts: a higher and a lower pitch for females and a higher and a lower pitch for males. Hymns were meant to be sung at the tune comfortable to where a particular person's voice ranges. More and more, hymns are sung with only the highest female tune, which is the dominant melody. Contemporary songs usually have only two parts: the melody placed mid-range so that most people will be able to sing it, and the harmony part that is sung on-stage by a trained singer with a microphone so that the song sounds fuller. But what this does is rob the music of its full four-part richness, and make music much less interesting and participatory. It is no wonder that many people do not feel comfortable singing in church. Most people are singing a dry melody at the wrong pitch.

At Family of Faith Church, we are trying to reintroduce hymn singing. Each family gets a home-discipleship hymnbook of some of the most time-honored hymns, compiled by Doug Horne, a member of our church. He has also produced a CD that plays the accompaniment part with the melody, the alto, the tenor, and the bass parts played out separately. With these tools, families are encouraged to practice not only the hymn of the month, but to practice a particular part. On our own, or in a small family, it might not sound wonderful, but when we get together at our hymn sing, or at church, the sound is remarkable. This has been a great contribution to reintroducing hymn singing into Christian culture. (See Appendix A to learn more about the hymnbook and CD.)

A home-discipleship church says that what happens in the home is as important as what happens on Sunday, but in no way do we want to dilute the importance of what it means to be a church. We are a community in Christ—we pray and care for one another's burdens; we eat the Lord's Supper together; we pool our resources to make a difference in our neighborhoods and our world. We are stronger together than we can be on our own.

Part of what it means to be a church is to train one another in godly behavior, especially from generation to generation. A man named Dan heads up the men's ministry at Family of Faith Church, which meets once a month. Fathers are encouraged to bring their sons. At these well-attended meetings, there is teaching that supports men in their godly leadership and a practical activity for the training of sons.

We also see the church as a place for our young people to find each other for marriage. I have seen many pastors weighed down in their ministry by an unsupportive wife; I have seen many godly wives weighed down by the weak spiritual leadership that comes from their husband. In a home-discipleship church, we want to provide a place for young godly warriors to meet each other and form kingdom marriages. This role is a key one.

My son, Henry, met his wife in our home-discipleship church. When Tim, Sherri and their nine children started attending our church, we invited their family over to our home on hospitality Sunday. While we parents were encouraging each other in practicing discipleship in our homes, Henry and Melissa were talking about Israel's history. They clicked right away. What did Henry and Melissa need in order to make that "click" turn into a lifetime partnership? They needed opportunities for talking and listening to each other; our church offers a time for young people to get together, with parents included, to be trained in discipleship and to get confidence in meeting and getting to know each other. These meetings helped Henry and Melissa get to know each other more.

Another opportunity was when Henry decided he would teach New Testament Greek at our church. Tim and his three oldest daughters, including Melissa, signed up for the class. The Greek class met for eight months, giving another opportunity for Henry and Melissa to build the foundation of a kingdom marriage. By the time Melissa knew elementary Greek, Henry knew he was interested in her. Their courtship and engagement lasted three months, and they were married on July 16, 2005. Two home-discipleship families celebrated the kingdom union of their first-born children. That's what we want to have happen in home-discipleship churches!

We also desire to see the planting of home-discipleship churches in other places. We want to be kingdom-minded, to think not only of our own home or family or church but to look to other communities that can be touched with the power and passion of a strong walk with God. Wherever we see these church plantings, we hear stellar reports of what is happening. In Peoria, Illinois, Pastor Jesse Powell has planted a home-discipleship church. In just a couple of years, he has seen families practice home discipleship and the fruit it creates. One of the families that Pastor Powell has reached is Ruth and Brad. They were inspired greatly by the home-discipleship vision of Christian Leaders and their local Family of Faith Church in Peoria. Ruth wrote a reflection of what home discipleship has done in her life:

Twenty-five years ago, my dad described to his children an old-fashioned "camp meetin'": "Waayyy back about 100 years ago, people used to gather on hot summer evenings to worship God. Men would arrive early in the day to set up the huge tent. They covered the ground under the tent with a few inches of fresh sawdust, set up wooden chairs. After a potluck, families would wind their ways into the tent. Hymns of praise began the service. The traveling preacher would start in on a hell-fire-and-brimstone sermon. As the ending hymn played, people made their way to the front of the tent to meet Jesus."

After painting such a vivid word picture, Dad told us that WE were going to the camp meetin', that night at a place in our community that had been having meetings for 100 years! Our faces lit with excitement as we entered and saw the actual sawdust on the ground and the tent-top. Later on, the visiting pastor began to wrap up his thoughts on the dangers of hell. The organ music began. We waited. No one walked the sawdust trail to salvation that night.

In the car on the way home, we expressed our disappointment. My father assured us, "Perhaps tomorrow night someone will meet Christ. The important thing is to know that people DO walk the sawdust, with lives forever changed by an encounter with Christ."

I think what matters for me about that night twenty-five years ago is that my father took the time to set about in my life an excitement and expectation of the life-changing power of Jesus.

Home discipleship is exactly what I've been searching for to help me regain the excitement and expectation of a life-changing relationship with Jesus. The simplicity and practicality of talking and listening to God every day with my children, with my spouse, and by myself really resonated. Both the *Christian Leaders Family Journal* and the encouragement of the Peoria Family of Faith Church have made a big difference in my life. I've been very thankful for the joy, hope, strength, and direction I find in the Word, and am equally excited about sharing these with others.

Brad has left his well-paying job at Caterpillar to teach English in Mongolia. He and Ruth along with their family are walking the discipleship sawdust trail.

Much of this book will deal with the underlying principles of home discipleship and at times might feel philosophical or heavy. But know that in practice, it does not feel heavy. You might not have a Brad and Ruth in your congregation, but you will have your own people who catch the vision and run with it. You will find people who amaze you with their unexpected memorization of Scripture, or tone-deaf people who suddenly figure out how to sing. You will discover people who motivate you or flat-out surprise you with their enthusiasm or perseverance.

At my church there is a man, Phil, who at age 60 has just started hospice. He has Huntington's disease, a genetic disease that slowly affects motor movements including walking, balance, and talking. In the later stages, it affects reasoning and short-term memory. For the last three years, Phil has slowly been declining and is now consigned to a wheelchair. He and his wife, Chery, have dealt with the disease by staying close to the Lord. One of the things that has been so encouraging to the whole church and their children is to see Phil participate in memorizing Scripture even though the disease is in the advanced stages. When I see Phil and Chery with their youngest daughter, Julie, get in front of everyone and recite a passage, it inspires me to lead my own family to memorize Scripture. Phil may not be able to walk or carry a clear conversation, but the Word of God still is spoken out of his lips with his family.

It is one thing to understand that a home-discipleship church reaches and supports people who desire to be players, not spectators, in their daily walks with God—but it is another thing entirely to experience it. My intention in writing this chapter is not to brag about my church, but to let you know up front that these principles work. They work in the lives of real people, real families with the same dilemmas and schedules as yours. I hope this taste of the end result will inspire you to keep reading, maybe even light a fire for your role in spreading Christianity—starting in your own life and family and extending your impact to as far as possible. I am hoping that some of you call me after you read this book and inquire about how our church has used family journals or hymnbooks. I am hoping that some of you will ask to enroll in the Christian Leaders Institute and earn a certificate in home-discipleship church planting and pastoring. I am hoping that you will develop a walk with God in your family that spreads spontaneously.

Chapter 2

Christian Branding:
The Seven Connections to God

HOME-DISCIPLESHIP Christianity involves every aspect of your life and the life of your family. It touches how you think, how you speak, how you work, how you worship. It is not something you can squeeze into the corner of your calendar; it's the very framework into which you slot the events of your life. It asks you to incorporate your walk with God into everything you do.

Perhaps this sounds a little too intense. Perhaps you think it unrealistic that ordinary Christians would give over so much of their time and commitments to spiritual development. In a nation where even devoted Christians often fulfill only the bare minimum of church attendance, is the all-consuming approach of home-discipleship Christianity just a pipe dream?

Put simply, no. Unless you and I are consumed by Christ, we will be consumed by something else. Each of us orients our lives around something, and if we do not make it our walk with God, then it will be our walk in the world. We are in a competition with the advertisers of this world, who want to sell to us a particular kind of lifestyle. They want us to spend, they want us to be busy, they want us to shortchange our personal relationships and fit in religion on the fringes. If we believe that any areas of our life are exempt from influencing our relationship with God, we are mistaken. Every choice we make affects who we become. This is something the advertisers of Madison Avenue know full well.

A few years ago, a colleague of mine attended a cultural-branding seminar, put on by the top marketing minds in America, and the report he gave me was troubling on many levels. When asked to think about the term "branding," I thought of slogans such as "Coke is the real thing." But that's only a small part of how the industry thinks of branding now. The way they are doing branding now is "behavior branding." Instead of merely selling a brand, the marketers are selling the *behavior* that sells product. For instance, it is just as important to market the behavior of drinking flavored carbonated sugar water. Then the soft drink maker can position its products around more people who drink pop.

The marketers have also been analyzing lifestyle behaviors. This could be called "cultural branding." Certain lifestyles and habits are more lucrative than others are. For example, a divorced home creates more business than a home where the father and mother stay together. A single lifestyle sells more product than a happily married lifestyle. An MTV marketing executive said that the lifestyle where sex is outside of marriage sells more beer than sex inside the bounds of marriage. The marketing industry has a lot of say in the media industry. Marketers are now consulted as to which programs or movies are watched in the media. Marketers weigh in as to what stories are told in our culture.

What stories are told? They tell stories where over 90 percent of the sex scenes are not in the bounds of marriage. Marriage is usually depicted as boring and dull. They tell stories where violence and death are commonplace, stories that sell despair and loneliness, stories that include homosexuality as a positive sexual lifestyle, stories that show fathers as weak or as womanizers, and mothers as two-career super-creatures or as "desperate" housewives. The family is not depicted as the traditional stable family, but as weak and out of control. You hardly see a movie that has the family opening a meal with prayer. Maybe you'll see a Hallmark movie showing a family of a hundred years ago that conducted family devotions. Today, Christianity is usually portrayed as either watered-down liberalism or as extreme unrealistic fundamentalism. If a movie depicts Christianity as warm and sincere, the critics call it "Pollyanna" and it is only sparsely attended.

"Faith in a Box: Entertainment Television and Religion," a study conducted in 1994 by the Los Angeles-based council in conjunction with the National Religious Broadcasters, found that the media ordinarily depicts faith in a negative light. NBC, for example, portrayed 9.5 negative treatments of faith for every positive treatment. In other words, the media is supporting a cultural branding that is unfriendly to walking with God.

> American advertisers spend about US $700 million annually advertising to kids. TV is by far the favored medium for advertising to children, accounting for over US $350 million worth of advertising dollars. (Milton Chen, *Smart Parents' Guide to Kids TV*, San Francisco: KQED Books, 1994)

One of the marketing executives at the cultural-branding conference specifically mentioned breaking down traditional values. He had graphs and charts describing the habits and behaviors that sell the most products. For instance: Individuals alone or divorces are more lucrative than lifelong married couples. The amount of money made from those who practice the homosexual lifestyle is greater than straight singles. The list went on. It was clear that the Christian worldview is not the most lucrative lifestyle or culture. Near the end of his comments, a slight residue of religion raised it head. He rhetorically questioned whether or not it was immoral to work actively against traditional values. His conclusion: "I'm not immoral, I'm greedy." This sounds similar to the gist of Revelation 18. In this passage, judgment is meted out in preparation for the last battle depicted in the next chapter.

> The merchants of the earth will weep and mourn over her because no one buys their cargoes any more—cargoes of gold, silver, precious stones and pearls; fine linen, purple, silk and scarlet cloth; every sort of citron wood, and articles of every kind made of ivory, costly wood, bronze, iron and marble; cargoes of cinnamon and spice, of incense, myrrh and frankincense, of wine and olive oil, of fine flour and wheat; cattle and sheep; horses and carriages; and *bodies and souls of men.* (Revelation 18:11-13, italics added)

Cultural branding is not delivered to us through reasoned arguments or friendly debates on an issue. Cultural branding is more insidious. It simply wants you to assume that the cultural landscape that the media presents is normal; it doesn't need to convince you that you, personally, should get a divorce, but it convinces you that "that's the way things are" and to turn a blind eye to couples having trouble or considering divorce. The primary weapon of cultural branding is time; the more time you spend plugged into the mega-billion dollar "entertainment" and media industry, the more likely you are to buy non-Christian definitions of the family. You are more likely to want to consume the products that the world is selling. You are more likely to become desensitized and discontented.

In the battle for your time, it is difficult to gauge whether you are winning or losing. Here's why: The use of your time usually does not submit to the same scrutiny as your evaluation of ideas and specific lifestyles. Let's say you found a TV that displayed only "good" programming. If you spent five hours a day watching good programs, it might still be harmful to you. Your life might still abound with the things of humanity. Your habits center on things of the world, even if they might be "decent." The same thing can happen to people watching or playing sports. Sports are not bad in themselves. But if sports dominate your schedule to the point that everything else is bullied out of your life, you have become culturally branded as a sports person.

I don't know which is more dangerous, the mind and heart side of cultural branding or the time side. I do believe that Satan wants to brand our mind, lifestyle, and culture to conform to the "pattern" of the world. Maybe the mark of the beast talked about in Revelation is the branding of the beast—branding your mind and time to center on humanity and not center on God.

Humans cannot avoid a form of cultural branding. We have a pattern of doing things. We have habits and sets of ideas. We create culture based on the choices we make in living out the patterns of our lives. The challenge is to become self-aware of the pattern or branding in your life. If you have to be branded with something, it should be something that you consciously make a decision to accept, not simply what the world forces on you. The apostle Paul urged believers:

> Do not conform any longer to the pattern of this world, but be transformed by the renewing of your mind. Then you will be able to test and approve what God's will is—his good, pleasing and perfect will. (Romans 12:2)

The pattern of our lives as followers of Jesus is to be structured in such a way that God is the center of your existence. Your relationship with God—that back-and-forth, conversational, and ever-deepening relationship—has to be your number-one priority. Since God desires nurturing, loving relationships between human beings, your second priority is to value all of your human relationships—with friends, with family, with neighbors, with people in your church, with people who have never set foot in a church. The branding of home-discipleship Christianity asks you to consider whom you are spending your time with, what your purpose together is, and how God is revealed in that relationship. It takes seriously the commandments to "love the Lord your God" and "love your neighbor as yourself," and asks you to take practical steps toward those aims each and every day.

The Heart of Home-Discipleship Christianity

How does a human being connect to God? In what ways does God reveal himself to us, and how do we speak back to him? The Sunday church service is probably the number-one way that most Christians carry out this back-and-forth conversation with God. Together we sing our praises to God, and a preacher speaks the Word of God into our lives. A secondary method many Christians use is the habit of personal devotions, usually consisting of prayer and Bible reading. Corporate worship and personal devotions both offer different experiences of God. In the former, we are strengthened by the solidarity of being the body of Christ, bringing the many gifts of the community before God, greeting, exhorting, singing, repenting, cleansing our hearts together. In the latter, we are one-on-one with God, hearing him speak clear direction into our situation, discovering how truly awesome he is, feeling him burn through the mask of our defenses to reach our inner helpless being. Neither church nor devotions are complete without the other, and neither is a substitute for the other.

In most Christian circles, attending church and having personal devotions each morning is where the bar is set in terms of having a deep connection with God. But there are so many other ways in which God can connect if we let him into all of our human relationships. The family is one of the key areas that we have lost this joint pursuit of God as churches have launched specialized programs for each family member. But a few generations ago, it was considered common practice for a family to gather around the dinner table, read and discuss the Bible, and pray together. How might we experience God more fully if we reinstituted this practice? As parents, we can learn a lot about the Bible and about God by teaching to our children. There are many things we might take for granted about our faith that can be reawakened by young people traveling that journey toward claiming faith for their own. There are a lot of habits in our lives that we might reexamine if we know that our children are watching us to see how to behave as a Christian. There are moments of frustration with children that can be diffused by a consistent habit of bringing our burdens before God together.

What about our marriages? God says that he is present when two or more people gather in his name, so anytime a husband and wife set aside time to approach God together, he is there for them. How would it affect our marriages if we made daily devotions a center of our relationship? What would happen if we had to be honest with God in front of our spouses? What would happen if we received God's grace and passed it on to each other? What if our goal as a couple was to enter more fully into God's presence?

There are other ways of connecting to God that we might not have considered. What about our relationship with the kingdom of God around the world? What would happen if we sat down to talk with other believers from different denominations or different countries and shared our experiences of God? What would we learn about the ways that God works in the lives of his people? What would happen if we sang together, prayed together? What if we encouraged each other to keep spreading the gospel message, to keep battling back Satan's attempts to grip the church in divisiveness?

What about our relationships with non-Christians? It might seem counterintuitive to say that we can learn something about God from people who don't believe in him. But the more we talk about our faith with those who don't agree, the deeper it can become. We can marvel at the incredible love of God who cares for all human beings no matter how much they have wronged him. We can be reminded how precious our faith is to us instead of taking it for granted. We can learn how to explain our love of God in ways that make sense to those who are on the seeking path. When we take on a mentoring relationship with someone and lead that person to Christ, we can experience something of God's power that is wholly unique.

What about mentoring relationships with like-minded Christians, people who are going to keep you on track with your goals and offer you accountability? What about regular small-group church meetings, Friday night barbeques with extended family, camping trips with neighbors? What would happen if we lived life openly and up close with like-minded believers? How might God enter into our lives as we stumbled and fell and were picked up by someone who loves us as Christ does? How might we experience God as we learn hymns together, break bread, pray for each other, create traditions, and watch each other grow and mature over years and decades?

These seven connections—our personal, marriage, family, fellowship, church, kingdom, and world connections to God—are the heart of home-discipleship Christianity. If we can bring God into the center of each of these relationships, then we will be branded by God and not by the world. As we create habits that ensure we are keeping God at the center, we have the tools necessary to share this incredible relationship with God and to help a person begin one as well. This is how home-discipleship Christianity spreads spontaneously, not by an effort to convert or change someone else's heart, but by changing your own heart and your own habits to bring God to the center of all your relationships. If God is present in your connection with another person, that relationship cannot help but change and alter as his grace and love works its way inside.

It might seem like a lot of work to keep track of seven different connections, to juggle all the priorities that they might demand of you. But they are really very simple. There is only one priority you need to have, only one habit you need to learn: the habit of talking and listening. Every relationship forms through a habit of talking and listening to another person. When you stop listening to people, you cannot relate with them. When you don't talk to people, they lose touch with you. It is a habit of consistent, repeated talking and listening that makes a relationship grow. So in each connection, we have to ask ourselves: How can we bring a habit of talking and listening to God in the midst of our time together?

Connection One—Personal Life

There are many ways a person can hear God's voice. God can speak of his glory through the spectacular sunset or the splendor of the oak tree in your backyard. He can speak to us in dreams, in the events of our lives, through work, through rest, through the exercise of our creativity. But the most reliable, consistent method of hearing from God is to read the Bible, his Word to us. This is a method that can be passed on to anyone; it is a method that every Christian must encounter at one point or another. In the same way, we can speak to God through song and poetry, in recited prayers and just plain speech. All of these are forms of prayer. I recommend choosing a prayer guide, or a regular pattern for talking to God, so that you will continue to talk to God no matter what your energy level or schedule is like on a particular day. This also gives you something concrete to pass along to someone you disciple.

A Bible-reading habit and a prayer guide do not equal a walk with God. They are just tools to help keep your walk with God on its feet. Our walk with God is an active, back-and-forth relationship in which we "work out our salvation with fear and trembling" (Philippians 2:12). It is in this relationship, in this familiar walk with God, that we are saved as we cry out for mercy to the almighty and all-forgiving God. We are not saved by the "good works" of Bible reading and prayer. We encourage them as a way of creating an intentional walk with God that will last through life's ups and downs. It is similar to asking a family to eat their meals together—sitting down together does not make you a family, but it is much harder to be a family without the habit of sitting down together.

Why is it important to have a personal relationship with God? Because God already relates to each of us personally. He created each one of us uniquely and loves us deeply. At the end of our lives, the Bible says, each of us must give an account to God (Romans 14:12). You may not want to talk and listen to God, but God sees you and you will someday stand individually before him. The gospel is that you and I can walk with God in Christ Jesus out of a relationship established from grace. The Holy Spirit now blows on us to make us born again. This relationship is to be real and vital as an individual realizes that he or she is relating honestly to the God of the universe.

Connection Two—Marriage

What does a marriage connection with God look like? The heart of a marriage connection is a devotional life that fully involves both spouses. It is setting aside time to read from the Bible together, to discuss and learn from the passage together, to pray openly before God together, to bring all your joys, your concerns, your repentances. Doing marriage devotions is an acknowledgement that you have been joined together in the eyes of God and that you want to please him with your relationship and your habits together.

God sees a married couple as one flesh. "The two shall become one," the Bible says (Genesis 2:24; Matthew 19:5), and Christian marriage partners are held accountable together on this earth. When the early church was just starting out, there were a husband and wife named Ananias and Sapphira who lied to the Holy Spirit about a piece of land they had sold (Acts 5:1-11). God held both of them accountable for their sin. He considered Ananias and Sapphira as one entity. Earlier in the Bible, God held Adam and Eve together accountable (Genesis 3). Christian marriages relate directly to the Lord. The culture of talking and listening repeatedly with God is something that will help Christians who marry. The apostle Paul encouraged those who marry to submit to and love each other in a relationship "in the Lord" (Colossians 3:18-19).

When God is a central player in your marriage, your marriage will benefit greatly from God's presence and guidance.

Connection Three—Family

God also relates to families. The biblical evidence is extensive. God related to Abraham, Isaac, and Jacob, creating a covenant with their family line to make their descendants a great nation. When a Christian has a baby, even that baby relates to God through the family. Does it mean that the baby is automatically saved? No. But the parents raise and nurture that child with the realization that the child belongs to God. God relates to families, not just individuals. Because the child belongs to God, Christian parents are called to disciple that child and any more children they are blessed with.

This connection is where home-discipleship Christianity finds a strong foundation. As you work together as a family to connect to God, you learn so much about how to discipline yourself to seek God, how to explain God in ways that others can understand, and how God transforms the relationships that you have with each other. This is a primary reason that home-discipleship Christianity spreads spontaneously—others can see firsthand what a difference God makes in your lives. The home lives of many who don't know God are filled with tension, bitterness, anger, argument, and failure, because each member of the family is striving for a separate agenda, for personal needs and desires. A family that is striving to fulfill God's will and God's direction is unified along one goal. This is an attractive model to those without direction. A family that has certain habits designed to put God at the center can offer to disciple another family easily, passing along the habits and letting God work his way into the relationships in other families.

In this selfish and egocentric world, individuals are often unreceptive to the idea that they are sinful and need to change. Most people think of themselves as basically good people. But in people's broken relationships with one another, in the midst of family conflict and strife, in destructive marriages, they come to understand that something needs to change. They are looking for answers—they are looking for people who model a functional family home and a loving marriage—and that is the place where we are best able to introduce the grace of God into their lives.

What does a family connection with God look like? Again, it is the basic habits of reading the Bible together and praying together. When your family takes time to listen to God and talk to God together through family devotions, your family grows spiritually. You might hold a weekly family meeting. At the family meeting, you can recognize individual family members in their walks with God. Maybe a child met a memorization goal. At the family level, children can see the roles of the father and mother as models of discipleship. Other elements might include family memorization and family singing, habits that make it easier for other families who want a better family life to join you and pursue the same goal.

Connection Four—Fellowship

In the past, families usually lived close to each other. Elderly parents stayed with their children. The Christian family unit expanded and had a support role for connections one, two, and three. When I grew up in the 1960s, all my relatives gathered at our home after church for coffee and cake. My grandma was there. My aunts and uncles were there. They talked about the weather. But they also talked about God. We often read the Bible and sang hymns. At Christmas we had an extended family program where the little kids acted out the Christmas story. There were godly poems read. Grandparents offered extended-family peer pressure whereby they expected every family to practice home discipleship.

The support of extended family is no longer available to many people today. Families do not have external motivation from loved ones to pursue personal, marriage, and family walks with God. Often extended families are not like-minded in their Christian values and home-discipleship practices. Therefore, today like-minded families need to find each other and gather to support one another in practicing home discipleship. Many churches have started small groups or Bible studies that provide support.

However you fulfill this fellowship connection—through extended family, small-group gatherings, neighborhood accountability meetings, and so forth—what is important is the habits of talking to God together through prayer and listening to God together through Bible reading. We experience encouragement with a large group of peers through which we can be honest about the ups and downs of our walks with God. We experience the freedom to admit that we don't have it all together, and yet we are also there to push each other onward in getting closer to God. A vital Christian needs the support of a fellowship connection. We need that opportunity to be accountable with like-minded Christian friends in an intimate way that isn't always possible at our gatherings for Sunday worship.

Connection Five—Church

Church is another way of talking and listening to God that connects us with a wider body of believers. I grant you that it is often a complicated form of talking and listening. A song could be a prayer or praise—a form of talking to God. A song could be a proclamation of God's Word: "Amazing grace, how sweet the sound." The preaching of the Word is a more extensive expression of simply opening the Bible. The sacraments are at their essence a proclamation of the Word. While the other four connections have elements of our own personality and our tastes reflected in how we construct them, the church service is a submission to someone else's planning, and we experience God in a broader way that involves more and more of his believers. A talking-and-listening dialogue with God is at the heart of corporate worship.

The role of church in the support of a believer's walk is an important discussion. If the sum total of someone's walk with God is showing up at church, that person will not likely grow deeply in a relationship with God. Also, churches today are setting up programs that do not necessarily support the family, marriages, and individuals in their walks with God. Instead, the many programs have fragmented families in an attempt to reach individuals.

A home-discipleship church attempts to support the previous four connections—like-minded fellowship, family gathering, marriage life, and an individual's relationship with God. A home-discipleship church builds a culture of home discipleship and gives a forum to recognize its advancement. A home-discipleship church does not seek to bring in better musicians, better evangelists, or better speakers, but seeks to grow and develop from within an entire church of people who practice singing, who practice sharing their faith, who practice reading in front of the church. A home-discipleship church says that, rather than dividing labor so that people serve only where they are gifted, everyone in the church is playing the same game and experiencing the fullness of all the ways in which human beings can serve God.

Connection Six—Kingdom

The kingdom of God exceeds and transcends any one church. There are layers and layers of networks that support the works of each church, from the seminaries that train the next generation of leaders to the Christian book publishers that offer materials that can inform and support our spiritual habits. There are denominations, missionary organizations, Christian colleges, home-school support organizations, news magazines, church associations, and many other networks that all work toward making the grassroots local churches function well.

It can be very easy to turn our relationship with the kingdom of God into only a listening relationship. We buy the products and read the books; we attend classes and peruse the newsletters. But if we are to have a talking-and-listening relationship with the larger kingdom, it means being involved in some of these organizations, speaking up about the direction they're headed, creating new networks to support the values you hold. It means talking and listening to God with allies and dreaming big about what God can do with you.

There are many friends of the home-discipleship movement in

the larger kingdom, and we want our churches and families to invest in strengthening these networks. In the past, denominations were the central organizations that supported large numbers of like-minded churches and families that were all on a common path. This dynamic is changing. Often people are encouraged by parachurch organizations that support the values of a particular church or family: For example, Christian-school families or home-schooling families "feel" a unity with others who have made similar school choices. Colleges often support these like-minded families; Calvin College, Trinity, and Dordt College are home to mostly Christian-school students, and Patrick Henry College has a large Christian home-school demographic. Parachurch organizations will provide a crucial role in the advancement of a home-discipleship culture.

At the same time, the kingdom of God incorporates many folks who are not like-minded, and we can benefit much from these relationships as well. Just as iron sharpens iron, we will hone and strengthen our walks with God when we submit ourselves and our churches to the scrutiny of others. As a home-discipleship church, we should always ask others to make sure that we are not just reciting Scripture and memorizing songs for mere spiritual achievement but that it's truly doing God's work in our lives. One of the dangers of any sort of habit is that at some point it loses its meaning and becomes just a rote exercise, and we need people to challenge us in that. At the same time, we have a responsibility toward other associations and organizations to hold them accountable: that the Christian media is pursuing more than just profit, that Christian schools have high standards of scholarship and integrity, that our denominations continue to uphold our values and traditions.

A kingdom connection might be as simple as two friends sitting down together over a cup of coffee, sharing what is going on at their respective churches. It might be going on a short-term missions trip to learn how people in a different country worship God. A kingdom connection is admitting that, despite a hope that we might be able to grasp the fullness of God in our local church, God is bigger than our small slice of the world, and we can learn something from one another. It is saying: Let's talk and listen to God together and see where he is leading us.

Connection Seven—World

Evangelism is often approached by the church as a presentation of the gospel ending in an offer to pray the sinner's prayer. But if we take the idea of a talking and listening relationship with God and apply it to the world outside God's kingdom, it immediately suggests a different approach. When we think of home-discipleship evangelism, we think of the word *leadership*. We desire to lead a person into a walk with God. While it is important to help them profess with their mouth that Jesus is Lord and Savior, home-discipleship evangelism seeks to reproduce not only a sinner's prayer but also a saintly walk.

The way in which someone is introduced to Jesus Christ has long-lasting impact on his or her Christian faith. If a person's first taste of the hope and redemption of Jesus came at a spiritual retreat, for instance, often that person will seek out retreats and seminars to get back that spiritual "high" when things are tough. If a person came to faith after hearing an amazing preacher, he or she will try to share the gospel by letting a pastor or a video do the talking. If a person was scared into believing in Jesus, it might take years or a lifetime to understand salvation as a loving and free gift.

The home-discipleship form of evangelism—inviting people to participate in talking and listening to God alongside you—is a daily, stable, relational, Scriptural, and reproducible entry into the Christian faith. It establishes a healthy spiritual DNA, creating habits that can be returned to again and again and that can be passed on. What's more, it doesn't take any special talent or training, just a willingness to do what you do in your everyday life with someone else. It is a chance to connect to God in a unique way, seeing things through the eyes of a newcomer or skeptic and really shedding light on the true privilege we have to be in a living relationship with the creator of all that is.

Creating a Culture

As Christians, we need to be very deliberate about the behaviors and patterns of our lives. If we don't intentionally live out the behaviors and patterns handed down through the Bible, our lives may look more like what the marketers want. The battle is for the attitudes and habits of the heart. If you can get people to watch eight hours of TV in a day, you can sell them something. They will become loyal to your product. Their lifestyle will reflect their loyalties and habits. And those habits and loyalties will be reproduced in their circle of influence. Who someone really is can usually be seen in how someone lives.

The pattern of our lives needs to be a godly and biblical branding, a branding that puts God's imprint on every aspect of our lives. This branding needs reinforcement through God-centered ideas and habits. This branding needs to be upheld and contributed to by the people around us. What we really need is a culture of people who are willing to make God the center of our lives—a God culture.

The goal of a home-discipleship church is to create a God culture. That's the measuring stick we use for success, not the number of songs a person memorizes or how many people someone invites over. The seven connections are not a checklist but a way of thinking about the world that says that any moment in any relationship can be an opportunity to meet God together. The seven connections prompt us to surround ourselves with people who are after the same vibrant walk with God we want. Our desire is to live in a Christian culture that reflects the values, knowledge, and habits of people in a relationship with God.

Rich DeVos taught me that if you have a big dream, and you are willing to habitually do the things you need to do to grasp that dream, then you can realize that dream. Rich used to tell me that success is not one big excellent decision. It is small decisions that are good. And when enough small decisions add up, you put yourself in the ballpark of success. A walk with God is a daily thing; it includes yourself, your spouse (if you are married), and your family. God usually does not show up to you in a burning bush, but over time you sense and know his presence. Over time your life and relationships transform by the power of God.

As you live this way, others will see your spiritual confidence. They will see the joy you have. They will want to find out what makes you different. And you will have something to share. You will share your spiritual dream. You will share the habits and lifestyle that keep you close to God. You will show them that even if everyone around you is selling despair, you are not buying. You are a person with a spiritual compass. God will use you to change your family and the world.

Chapter 3

Connection Seven: Home-Discipleship Evangelism

IT IS important to understand that the seven connections are not seven separate disciplines. They are a single discipline— talking and listening to God—lived out in seven contexts with different groups of people. The objective is not to work out your personal connection with God to complete fulfillment and then move on to the next challenge. You need all seven connections at once; one of the ways in which you can succeed at a personal connection with God is to take the responsibility of leading your family in a walk with God, reaching out to other families, and receiving support in a culture of walking with God. In the same way, a church connection with God and a marriage connection with God are not a substitute for your own individual walk with God.

To drive that point home, we'll begin our deeper look at the connections with the last on the list: evangelism, or our world connection. It's important, as we explain the basic truths of Christian belief, that we communicate that faith is a relationship. Faith is not simply agreement with a list of propositions. Faith is not a ticket to heaven or an insurance policy. Faith is an ongoing search for the heart of God, a desire to draw near and be transformed by his overwhelming holiness and unbridled love until we are more like him. This happens only in a relationship—by talking and listening day by day, by going through times of distance and closeness, by developing a history together that we can come to trust. This chapter will be key because without the idea of relationship, all seven connections will seem like an obligation of rote spiritual exercises. Home discipleship succeeds or fails depending on a proper understanding of relationship and how our daily spiritual habits lead us to renewed joy in that connection with God.

Sharing the Relationship

Jason and Ashley Smith are in their mid-thirties and have been married for 10 years. They have four children, and they want more. Jason and Ashley found a home-discipleship church. Their family is growing close to God and close to each other; they are delighted with what is happening in their family. Their usual pattern is daily to read the Bible for at least five minutes as a family, then memorize Scripture together and sing a hymn of the month. At church the pastor preaches on what they are reading at home. The church also sings the hymn of the month along with some contemporary songs. Once a month, the church provides an opportunity for the family to recite the memorized verses. Jason and Ashley go to a church that actually supports the success of the home. The church lets the children stay with the parents. Jason and Ashley hope that their children will find their spouses in this church someday.

This journey to a home-discipleship church is a recent development for Jason and Ashley. As children they rarely attended church. They were each raised by a father and mother who both had to work, and Jason and Ashley both wanted careers as well. They got great jobs right out of college, Jason as a sales manager and Ashley working for a prestigious law firm. They bought a modest starter home. Jason and Ashley planned not to have children right away but to wait about 7 years so they could become well established.

Shock would be an understatement: Birth control did not work. Ashley was pregnant after eight months of marriage, and was soon overwhelmed by little Amber. A neighbor with eight children offered to help out, and Ashley was amazed at what she saw next door. One child felt daunting, but the Lockheeds seemed so happy with eight. Sarah Lockheed taught Ashley the secrets of mothering, and Sarah's daughters attended to Amber whenever they got a chance. Ashley thought of a great idea: After her pregnancy leave, she could pay the Lockheeds to take care of Amber. Much to her happiness, the Lockheeds accepted. Sarah said that taking Amber would be no trouble. She also said, "Forget about giving us any pay."

Ashley was intrigued by the Lockheeds' vision of the world. John Lockheed worked hard to support his wife and children. John was a gracious and visionary guy. Ashley could tell that John and Sarah had a great marriage. Ashley had to admit to herself that at first she did not believe that traditional families still existed.

Ashley loved picking up Amber after work. She loved seeing the family in operation; she liked what she saw in the Lockheed children. Those children loved being with each other, and they really had joy. She started asking Sarah about her opinions: Why are you having so many children? Why did you decide to be a traditional family?

Sarah explained that when she and John first married, she firmly believed in women's lib, and John was a "forward" thinker who loathed anything to do with family values. After living together for a couple of years, they decided to get married because they both liked a particular house and they figured that getting married would allow them to afford it. After a year of marriage, they were at the verge of splitting when they heard the message of Christianity. They both turned from their lost ways and followed Christ. The person who introduced them to Christ also introduced them to Bible-reading and prayer practices.

After a year of reading the Bible together, attending church, and being mentored by this Christian friend, John and Sarah were developing a strong relationship with Christ. Soon children followed, and that pattern of home discipleship enriched their family life greatly. They started home schooling because they found this the simplest lifestyle for maintaining excellent prayer and Bible-reading habits.

When Jason and Ashley came into John and Sarah's life, John and Sarah were maturing Christians involved with other believers in founding a home-discipleship group. This group had become a home-discipleship church. Many families had come together to support each other in doing home discipleship.

One day John and Sarah invited Jason and Ashley to dinner. Something unusual occurred: After the meal, the Lockheeds opened the Bible and read it for a few minutes. They also spent five minutes doing a Bible-memory passage. Much to their surprise, their daughter Amber was saying the passage out loud with the Lockheed family. Impressed, Jason asked some questions about the Bible. John answered as best he could and invited Jason and Ashley to their church's hymn sing. They asked permission if Amber could accompany the Lockheed family in reciting a Bible passage. Jason and Ashley agreed. The meal concluded with a hymn that Amber sang along to. Jason and Ashley watched.

At the hymn sing, Jason and Ashley saw many other families recite Bible passages. They saw adults and children singing hymns. They sensed the presence of God in the eyes of those participating.

Jason and Ashley asked John and Sarah many questions about Christianity and soon decided that they wanted to begin a relationship with Christ and practice home discipleship with Amber. They also reevaluated their stance on career goals and children; Ashley quit her job to stay home with their next addition. Jason and Ashley joined the Lockheeds' home-discipleship church, and they are now telling their family and friends about a home-discipleship relationship with God.

Evangelism Deficiencies

Most modern evangelism is event-based evangelism, wherein a potential believer is invited to a single evening to hear an often spectacular preacher share an emotion-based message. This method dates back to Charles Finney, who would assemble great crowds and preach with such passion before calling people forward to confess their sins. In the 20th century, Billy Sunday and Billy Graham are excellent examples of event-based evangelists. Radio and television ministries often have event-based evangelism features. Many churches now use front-door evangelism methods, designing a worship service to appeal specifically to seekers. Willow Creek Community Church has seeker services on the weekend, while believers go to mid-week services for discipleship. The strength of this style of evangelism is that you can reach large numbers of people in a short period. This method shows results on paper in a hurry and is primarily responsible for the excellent poll numbers concerning the percentage of people who have made a faith commitment to Jesus. Polls vary, but I keep reading that over 80 percent of Americans "believe" in Jesus. In many ways, event-based evangelism has done a great service by getting the word out that Jesus is a true historical figure, the Son of God, and that he must be taken seriously.

The weaknesses of this form of evangelism directly relate to the organizational and personnel choices necessary to execute this approach. One weakness concerns resources needed to pull it off. Here are some of the essential ingredients you need to do event-based evangelism:

1. Money (usually lots of it)
2. Very gifted speakers (well-known celebrities do very well)
3. High-tech media knowledge (high-end sound systems are vital)
4. Subtle cultural sensitivities (you must know what consumers really want)
5. Great numbers of Christian worker bees to be recruited, who will adopt this method and believe in the evangelistic style of the ministry
6. Training for the recruits that will elevate the specific organizational goals
7. An extensive form of follow-up (this is usually very difficult, making the follow-up rate of most event-based approaches quite dismal)

Another weakness of event-based evangelism is the fact that the show is everything. The organizers become like television producers who have a specific time to make a specific presentational pitch. New believers often make their decision related to the entertainment value of the production rather than its content. The show can look great even if the spiritual lives of the leaders are struggling. The larger the show, the more the demand on the leaders. This often brings leaders to an unbalanced lifestyle that is open to emotional and spiritual problems.

But the greatest deficiency of event-based evangelism concerns the nature of *how* someone hears about Christ. How people come to Christ forms a specific "DNA" that has lasting impact both for their spiritual growth and how they minister to others. Often in event-based evangelism, the goal is to help someone experience at that event a powerful spiritual pull toward God. While at one level this may be desired, at another level great caution must be exercised. If new believers understand that their walk with God is what they feel at that event, we have done them a great disservice. If new believers connect to God through an event leader's connection to God, we have done them a great disservice.

When a person attempts to develop a habit of personal devotions, prayer and Bible reading will often seem hollow in comparison with the entertaining event. As a married couple, each spouse could grow at different spiritual rates depending on the specific events each attends or does not attend. Since families include so many different ages and interests, the spiritual events have to be specifically targeted and still done well. One drop in excellence could mess up a family seeking to grow spiritually. This has led to the massive growth in what is called church shopping. Since people have been reached by events, and their walk with God is event-driven, many are continually looking for that which reaches the specific profile of their life and family. Church communities form less around encouraging each other in a full-orbed walk with God, but more and more around what the church or kingdom institution offers. And when people lose interest in that church or kingdom institution, they must look for another. That is in their DNA.

Home-Discipleship Evangelism

In home-discipleship evangelism, the costs are minimal. The staff is minimal. No specialized knowledge or extraordinary speakers are necessary. It's simply one family sharing with another family what it means to walk with God together.

This is a giant pressure off leaders who do not have to carry the weight of everyone's spiritual needs on their shoulders.

There is no pressure to be superhuman, only deeply human. They can work on leading and supporting, not on razzle-dazzle.

It sets the right spiritual DNA. Christianity is all about walking with God, and people are given the chance to see from the beginning what it's all about. There are no empty promises and emotional pulls but the honest truth of a life lived in faith. When a person's introduction to Christ happens in the context of a friendship, over a period of time, with exposure to the basic habits of Bible reading and prayer and a life among a community of believers, then it sets a DNA of direction, steadiness, wholeness, growth, connection, and commitment.

Home-discipleship evangelism is driven not by a sales pitch but by a share-what-you-do philosophy and a share-who-you-are approach. A person who practices home discipleship finds it natural to share about the family meeting and what's happening in the spiritual development of the family. It's a spontaneous desire to let others in on the secret rather than a forced presentation of a set of spiritual facts. On the other hand, the share-what-you-do approach always ends up at the question of *why* you do what you do, and it's important to have a grasp of the doctrine that drives the home-discipleship model. I want to spend the rest of the chapter explaining the gospel message in a progression that would make sense to someone who's seen home discipleship in action and is thinking about beginning a relationship with God. It will help set the spiritual DNA of a person who wants to receive salvation and carry it through to fruition in his or her actions. This section will be helpful to someone who is new to Christ, as well as to believers who want to better understand how home discipleship is an extension of the basic gospel message lived out day to day. The religious life is not an obligation imposed on us by a God who wants our obedience but an invitation into fulfillment of what he has planted most deeply in our souls.

The Spiritual Dream

I have asked this question hundreds of times in various parts of the world: "What is your spiritual dream?"

How would you answer it? Take a moment to stop reading and think about the question. Get a sheet of a paper and take three or four minutes to jot down some ideas.

There is something powerful about this question because many people think of their spiritual state as a yes-or-no kind of question: Either I am religious or irreligious. Either I am trying to pursue God or I don't really believe in him. Either I am in the kingdom of God or the kingdom of this world. To be able to name a spiritual dream means that you have purpose and direction, something to strive for and something to live for.

"What do you mean by spiritual?" most people ask, and I tell them to define it however they want. What are the hopes, ambitions, goals, and dreams you have for your life that are going to fulfill you on a deeper level?

By now most people have an idea of what I'm after, but are stumped by how to answer. We are not often taught to dream in a spiritual sense. What's more, if we define for ourselves a dream, then we have a certain obligation to fulfill it. Sometimes people are wary about speaking a dream out loud because often they know they have done nothing really to pursue it.

How about you? Have you come up with a dream yet? Was it something you'd really considered before? Does it sound daunting to put it down on paper?

"Anything at all," I reassure those who need further direction. "If you could have anything in the world." Once people get talking, I find it amazing how people give such very similar answers to this question. Most every answer falls into two categories:

Some will give an answer concerning their understanding of God. I have heard of answers like, "I want to be close to God," or "I want to be filled with the Holy Spirit even more." Some will say things like, "I want to be one with the whales." Although this is not strictly a God answer, a person who answers this way still has an inner prompting toward worshiping something beyond oneself.

Some will give answers concerning their relationships with people. I have heard of answers like, "I just want my kids to know God," or "I want to fight for my cause." One person told me he wanted to give down-and-out children boat rides paid for by the government. These answers are almost always about benefiting a specific person or a broad group of people whose lives will be made better.

Most spiritual dreams are in some way connected to worshiping a higher being and showing love to other people. It is interesting because the way most of us actually live out our lives is to benefit ourselves and enrich our own standing, but the moment we are asked to pay attention to our spiritual side, we gravitate toward looking outside ourselves. I like to start out with this question about spiritual dreams because it sets on the table two important desires that the average person has not fulfilled: connection with God and connection with people. I do not need to convince a person that he or she needs to have a spiritual life, because the person has just told me so in his or her own words. Suddenly the nice car and nice house aren't quite an adequate safeguard from needing something more.

Jesus of Nazareth taught that true fulfillment comes through a relationship with God, your creator, and through loving the people of this world. That's what the Christian life is all about— living out our spiritual dreams of worshipping the God of the universe and giving of ourselves to our friends and neighbors:

> One of the teachers of the law came and heard them debating.
> Noticing that Jesus had given them a good answer, he asked him,
> "Of all the commandments, which is the most important?" "The

most important one," answered Jesus, "is this: 'Hear, O Israel, the Lord our God, the Lord is one. Love the Lord your God with all your heart and with all your soul and with all your mind and with all your strength.' The second is this: 'Love your neighbor as yourself.' There is no commandment greater than these." (Mark 12:28-31)

God instilled in us our spiritual dreams, and he taught us how to pursue them by revealing himself as the one true God who deserves our worship and by revealing that every person we meet is a neighbor who deserves our love and attention. Many have rejected this call because it is too difficult. It can be easier to pop in a CD of whale calls or to throw money at a social program and pretend you are fulfilling a deeper connection. It feels like you have more control. What God asks of us is to give up control, to submit ourselves to the law of love—and by pursuing our dreams by his means rather than our own, we will find real fulfillment.

The Problem

Just because we each have a desire to worship and to love does not mean we are able to actually love God and our neighbor. The problem is that you and I were conceived in rebellion and sin (Psalm 51:5). We want to do things our own way, to be in control. This problem has plagued the human race since our first parents fell into sin (Genesis 3), and you and I are no different in our nature. The apostle Paul wrote in Romans 3:9-12:

> What shall we conclude then? Are we any better? Not at all! We have already made the charge that Jews and Gentiles alike are all under sin. As it is written: "There is no one righteous, not even one; there is no one who understands, no one who seeks God. All have turned away, they have together become worthless; there is no one who does good, not even one."

Complicating matters is that our fight is not just an internal struggle against our own rebellion and sin. Satan, or the devil, still has some power to deceive and blind humans. Paul wrote:

> The god of this age [Satan] has blinded the minds of unbelievers, so that they cannot see the light of the gospel of the glory of Christ, who is the image of God. (2 Corinthians 4:4)

Left to ourselves, you and I are lost! Yes, you have a spiritual dream. But sin has poisoned your nature against God and others, and Satan has blinded your eyes so that you do not see God. Even though you and I may "dream" of wanting God, left to our own power, you and I cannot lovingly relate to God.

The great news, the gospel of Christianity, is that God seeks to have a relationship of peace despite our wicked nature. God reverses what Satan has done.

Here is what is so amazing: God brings real forgiveness! The only thing that can free us from our selfish desires, our controlling ways, and our lack of love is forgiveness. We cannot pull up ourselves by our bootstraps and do better; we need to have this wickedness absolved in our lives, to experience the radiance of God's love and let ourselves be a vessel for carrying this love into the world. It is not we ourselves who learn to love, but we submit ourselves to experiencing and passing on the overflowing love of God.

Maybe you have a hard time believing that God could forgive you for what you have thought and done. Maybe your transgressions go deeper than just a selfish nature or a self-righteous attitude. You have thought very wicked thoughts against God and others. You have even acted wickedly. But God will forgive you and change your life. He has promised that no one is outside the reach of his redemption and transformative power.

Here is what is so amazing: God brings real goodness! Maybe you are from a Christian home, but you are not following God as your parents did. You consider yourself a "good" person; you were raised to be good. But deep down you know that you have not transferred the control of your life to God. You live according to the law but not according to the standard of love. But God will give you love; then the law will make sense.

Here is what is so amazing: God will take you where you are at now, and change you and restore or renew your spiritual dream! You will be vital in your walk with God. People in your life will see the change, and you will be involved in an eternal relationship. You have authority in Christ over Satan to be part of the building of the kingdom of God! You are saved from sin by the unbounded grace of God.

How is Grace Possible?

God is an absolutely perfect being. He cannot tolerate sin. When we hurt each other, when we turn our backs on what is decent and right and loving, he cannot possibly invite us into his presence. There is a wall that separates us. But even though you and I do not deserve it, God brought down the barrier out of sheer undeserved grace. When God's Son, Jesus, died on the cross, he took on himself all our sin. Jesus lived a perfect life yet was suffering the punishment for crimes he did not commit. He broke Satan's power over us. Because Jesus was fully God and fully human, the shedding of his blood meant complete forgiveness of believers' sin and restoration into new relationship. No more guilt, no more blindness. You and I are reconciled with God. Take note of these Scriptures:

> But God demonstrates his own love for us in this: While we were still sinners, Christ died for us. Since we have now been justified by his blood, how much more shall we be saved from God's wrath through him! (Romans 5:8-9)

> Here is a trustworthy saying that deserves full acceptance: Christ

Jesus came into the world to save sinners—of whom I am the worst. (1 Timothy 1:15)

All of us also lived among them at one time, gratifying the cravings of our sinful nature and following its desires and thoughts. Like the rest, we were by nature objects of wrath. But because of his great love for us, God, who is rich in mercy, made us alive with Christ even when we were dead in transgressions—it is by grace you have been saved. (Ephesians 2:3-5)

Submit yourselves, then, to God. Resist the devil, and he will flee from you. (James 4:7)

Will you still struggle with sin and temptation? Yes. Will you desire to run your own life rather than submit to God's plan for you? Yes. Sin is not absent, but more and more the changing power of God will make sin less desirable. Instead, we grow in attraction to a love of neighbor and worship of God. This lifelong process is called sanctification. Our old self passes away and God grants to us a new spirit, the Holy Spirit, which works within us to accomplish this process. Sin does not stand between God and us; rather he dwells in us and perfects us with his love.

Your Spiritual Dream Realized

Just because God has made possible this grace and offers it to us freely does not mean that we all have this grace in our lives. We must choose to receive his grace; we must accept his invitation into a relationship with him and accept the gift of a renewed heart that loves people. There is no magic formula to make these things happen, no words that unlock the secret door. There is only the surrender of the heart. There is the turn from our self-seeking ways to the will of God. There is the repentance of our sinful ways and the acceptance of forgiveness made possible by the death and resurrection of Jesus Christ. We die to ourselves and are reborn in the Holy Spirit of God.

Even though God looks at the heart and not at the words we recite, it can be helpful to walk through the process of salvation step by step and look at suggestions for what one might pray to God to receive his grace. This might be very basic if you have been a Christian for a long time, but read the next few pages in the spirit of a rededication of your life. Read also with the goal of helping a friend or neighbor come to know Christ. This process will not be so simple to a newcomer to the faith. Do not rush things by insisting right away on a commitment. Often a person will need to actually walk with God a while before deciding to commit his or her life to God. Simply share the steps and encourage the person to pray them whenever his or her heart is truly behind the words. Christian families have children who walk the walk for many years before they make their profession of faith, and home-discipleship evangelism takes the same approach: Explain the process of salvation, practice walking with God, and then give oneself up to God when God calls.

So much of this book will deal with the nuts and bolts of a daily reproducible walk with God. But know this: A daily walk comes out of a relationship that Jesus won for us. This relationship is a gift from God that we do not deserve. We might have a spiritual dream, but the dream would not make any sense without acknowledging God as the one who establishes a relationship with you and me, who makes all connection possible. Home discipleship, the seven connections, Bible reading, prayer, Sunday worship, the kingdom of God—all mean nothing without the foundational work of God saving us from the wages of sin and giving us new life in his Spirit.

Step One: Repent

Repenting is a turning to God and confessing that you are a sinner and that you need God in your life. Repenting is not

63

something you do lightly. This is something that you will continue to do throughout your Christian walk. Even when you come to the Lord's Supper, you will go with a repentant attitude. The Bible says:

> Repent, then, and turn to God, so that your sins may be wiped out, that times of refreshing may come from the Lord. (Acts 3:19)

A prayer of repentance: "Dear God in Heaven, I confess my willful rebellion against you. I have been in control of my own life. I freely desire to surrender my will. I pray these things in Jesus' name. Amen."

Step Two: Confess your Faith

In the Bible, the word *faith* is a relational word. When you become a believer, confessing your faith is like a groom saying his vows to his bride. Expressing your faith is a bold act of promise in your new relationship with God. The Bible says:

> That if you confess with your mouth, "Jesus is Lord," and believe in your heart that God raised him from the dead, you will be saved. For it is with your heart that you believe and are justified, and it is with your mouth that you confess and are saved. As the Scripture says, "Anyone who trusts in him will never be put to shame." For there is no difference between Jew and Gentile—the same Lord is Lord of all and richly blesses all who call on him, for, "Everyone who calls on the name of the Lord will be saved." (Romans 10:9-13)

This confession is not to be made lightly. You are now vowing to trust completely in God. You are entering into an eternal relationship. There is no turning back!

A prayer of belief: "Dear God, I trust in you as my Lord and my Savior. I receive from you your gracious gift of an eternal salvation, a relationship of peace from you, won for me by Jesus

Christ, when he suffered hell for me on the cross and when he rose again from the dead. I have been spiritually reborn as your child now. I now desire to serve you. I belong to you body and soul! In Jesus' name. Amen."

When you pray this prayer for the first time, you have just done something very bold. You have crossed over from death to life. You may not even feel like you did something that bold. If these prayers were truly from your heart, your spiritual center, you can be sure that you have been saved. Welcome to the body of believers!

One more thing about step two: Romans 10:9 says, "That if you confess with your mouth...." On one level, you did that today. You confessed your vow to God, between you and God. Now you need to confess your faith publicly. Just as marriage vows are made publicly, so it is with a confession of faith in Jesus. Maybe you have been nurtured in a Christian home. You do not remember a time when you did not trust in the Lord. For you maybe it is time to publicly declare your faith at your church. 2 Corinthians 4:13-15 puts it this way:

It is written: "I believed; therefore I have spoken." With that same spirit of faith we also believe and therefore speak, because we know that the one who raised the Lord Jesus from the dead will also raise us with Jesus and present us with you in his presence. All this is for your benefit, so that the grace that is reaching more and more people may cause thanksgiving to overflow to the glory of God.

Talk to the pastor at your church about being baptized or confirmed before the entire congregation. Baptism is the public acknowledgement that you accept God's gift of salvation and will live a new life in him.

Step Three: Walking in a Vital Relationship
When polls are conducted in America, over 80% of Americans

say that they believe in God. A large percentage of people even say that the Bible is God's Word. Many have confessed the sinner's prayer, a variation on what you may have just done in steps one and two. Yet the sad truth is that many who have professed their faith in Jesus do not walk daily with God in an ongoing transforming relationship. Many will attend church but fail to understand the relational nature of faith in Christ. They conclude that God/religion/church is a social event, a moral compass, a parenting and marriage guide, or social activism. While these things are natural by-products of a vital relationship, they are not the essence of walking with, serving, and loving God.

In realizing your spiritual dream to love God, you need to know basically who he *is*. He has revealed himself in history, and we can get to know him through his primary communication tool, the Bible. We call the Bible God's Word. You also need to know that you are relating to a spiritual being in trinity. The Bible points to one God in three persons: Father, Son, and Holy Spirit. In some ways, relating to a spiritual God is different from relating to other humans. In human history, small numbers of people have physically seen members of the Trinity, that is, God. Some have. Adam and Eve walked with God the Father in the Garden of Eden (Genesis 2-3). Moses saw a glimpse of God the Father at Mount Sinai:

> And the LORD said, "I will cause all my goodness to pass in front of you, and I will proclaim my name, the LORD, in your presence. I will have mercy on whom I will have mercy, and I will have compassion on whom I will have compassion. But," he said, "you cannot see my face, for no one may see me and live." Then the LORD said, "There is a place near me where you may stand on a rock. When my glory passes by, I will put you in a cleft in the rock and cover you with my hand until I have passed by. Then I will remove my hand and you will see my back; but my face must not

be seen." (Exodus 33:19-23)

The coming of Jesus, God's own son, put God in plain view. Jesus was fully God and fully human. By believing in Jesus, you are relating to God. Through the eyes of faith, you now "see" God. Hebrews 1:3 says:

> The Son is the radiance of God's glory and the exact representation of his being, sustaining all things by his powerful word. After he had provided purification for sins, he sat down at the right hand of the Majesty in heaven.

When Jesus was on this earth, he often spoke of the Holy Spirit. When Jesus was preparing to die on the cross, He promised the Holy Spirit:

> But the Counselor, the Holy Spirit, whom the Father will send in my name, will teach you all things and will remind you of everything I have said to you. (John 14:26)

The book of Acts from the Bible is often called the Acts of the Holy Spirit. The book of Acts shows how the Holy Spirit has been poured out to believers. This book shows that the Holy Spirit indwells believers. The person of the Holy Spirit empowers people to preach, to heal, to discern, to have authority over evil, and to receive special gifts to advance the Kingdom of God.

A very important creed in the early church was the Nicene Creed. This creed calls the Holy Spirit "the Lord and Giver of life; who proceeds from the Father and the Son; who with the Father and Son together is worshipped and glorified; who spake by the prophets." The Holy Spirit helps you "see" God!

When you professed your faith in Christ, you have come to God: Father, Son, and Holy Spirit. You have learned something very important now about the one you are relating to. You are not becoming one with the whales. You are not becoming one with the force. You connect directly to God. You do not need a human mediator. Jesus is your mediator:

> For there is one God and one mediator between God and men, the man Christ Jesus.... (1 Timothy 2:5)

You are connecting to the God of the universe revealed in the Bible. This is very different from relating to another human. This spiritual being, God, is distinct from his creation and creatures, yet we commune with God in an eternal love relationship. At the same time, relating to God is similar in many ways to relating to other humans. A relationship with God includes trust, love, service, loyalty, knowledge, etc. Just as human relationships have a key effect on our lives, a relationship with God has a major effect on our lives. Think of someone who married well; we may say that a wife really brings out the best in him or she really needs her husband. That same dynamic happens when you and I relate to God. Relating to God transforms us, changing the way we are in our marriage, our families, our friendship circles, our work, our communities, and our world. The fact is that God is *good* for us. He brings out the best in you and me. If you are teachable and open in this relationship, you are changed. God will change you through his communication tool, the Bible, and through his Holy Spirit, who now dwells in you as a believer.

There are other similarities between a relationship with God and human relationships. Another important one is the loving boundaries of your relationship with God. As you learn about God in the Bible, you will discover many of these boundaries. Human relationships have important boundaries; in marriage, it is between one man and one woman. I do not go home to another man's wife. I have my wife. I have promised to be faithful and loving to one woman. I do this out of love, not out of legalism. Out of love for us, God has set up certain boundaries. The Ten Commandments (Exodus 20) are an example of a wonderful

68

boundary. This boundary brings transforming power to our relationship with God and others. For instance, we cannot be loyal to God and chase after other gods, or idols, or anything other than God that captivates our spiritual passion. God is relationally jealous. He is not content to be one of many gods that we devote ourselves to any more than our spouse is content to be one of many husbands or wives.

Notice, too, that God sets up boundaries that help us love each other. We are told to honor our parents, to refrain from coveting anything our neighbors own, to keep from spreading falsehoods about others, to be faithful to our spouse. We are able with God's help to obtain our spiritual dreams in loving others. The Bible is filled with powerful encouragements and commands to act lovingly to our spouses, friends, families, and neighbors.

A prayer of wholehearted commitment: "Dear God—Father, Son and Holy Spirit—I desire a transforming and loving relationship with you! Father, I thank you that you made me and that you have given me your great compassion and grace. Jesus, I thank you for dying in my place. I owe my all to you. You are my Lord and Savior. Holy Spirit, fill me now with your presence. Guide me in my eternal relationship with God. Give me the power to actually walk with God daily and the boldness to share my walk with my family and others in my life. Help me to be used by you to build your eternal kingdom. In Jesus' name. Amen."

Home discipleship is all about this deep relationship. It's about giving us certain habits in our lives and certain frameworks that ensure that we pursue that relationship with everything we have. Attending church on Sundays is not going to do it. Having a few minutes of quiet time each day is not going to do it. Giving over our whole lives to God is what it takes—our time, attention, priorities, energy, and hearts. There is no keeping God at arm's length, no treating him like a genie whose bottle you rub whenever you get into trouble. God is your creator, your redeemer, and the source of all life and love. Let us explore more deeply how the habits and practices of home discipleship feed that eternal relationship and help it attain its fullness.

Chapter 4

Home-Discipleship Evangelism: Reproducing a Walk with God

I NOTICED her in the fall of 1981. I wanted to get to know her. She had her Sunday dress on, and she looked amazing. Her name was Pam Feddema. We grew up together in the same church. Our parents knew each other. She was quiet. I was loud. She knew how to listen. I knew how to talk. I was attracted to her. Why? I don't know.

> There are three things that are too amazing for me, four that I do not understand: the way of an eagle in the sky, the way of a snake on a rock, the way of a ship on the high seas, and the way of a man with a maiden. (Proverbs 30:18-19)

How was I going to get to know her? I could not form a relationship with her unless I found a way to talk and listen to her repeatedly. I needed to start a relational walk with her. Talking and listening repeatedly are the essential conversational elements in a relationship walk. Talking is important because in talking you reveal who you are. Listening is important because in listening you learn who the other person is. Doing them repeatedly is important because it takes time for talking and listening to develop familiarity and trust. The repeated aspects are the relationship habits or patterns. If those habits and patterns are weak, it will have an impact on the amount of talking and listening that occurs. This will lessen the levels of intimacy.

I eventually was able to take walks with Pam. Our courtship began. We took Sunday walks for several months. At first, she listened while I talked. At some point, she started talking while I listened. The pattern of talking and listening repeatedly was bearing fruit. Our repeated walks created levels of intimacy in two willing parties. It wasn't long before we were talking about marriage. We wed on June 4, 1983. We spoke our vows. Now, I have been talking and listening repeatedly to Pam for decades. The proximity of living together has helped to knit the pattern of talking and listening repeatedly into the very fabric of our lives. I habitually come home to Pam at our house.

Our walk of love today is still fed by talking and listening repeatedly. Most of the time, it just comes naturally to enter into conversation. "Hi honey, I'm home." "How was your day?" We do not have to remind ourselves to be interested in hearing from each other. In addition, though, we will schedule intentional time together, where we go on a trip together or specifically shut the bedroom door to focus on each other. The intentional times wouldn't go very well without the everyday talking and listening that's the lifeblood of the relationship, and yet without the occasional intentional focus on each other, the more familiar conversations might turn dry. Through both unprompted times of talking and listening as well as scheduled times of talking and listening, we prioritize these two central elements of a growing relationship.

With God, the pattern of communication is very similar. If you want to grow in a loving and profoundly satisfying relationship with God, you'll need to develop an excellent pattern of communication.

For thousands of years the relationship with God has been

called a "walk." A human walk brings people together for a journey. Pam and I took our Sunday afternoon walks. Have you ever been on a family walk? At the Reyenga home, we'll take walks quite frequently and we love them. A walk with God is about being in a regular proximity with him. Adam and Eve walked with God in the cool of the day (Genesis 3:8).

How does someone specifically walk with God today? A Christian walks with God in two aspects. Sometimes the difference between these aspects is hard to pin down. Generally speaking, we walk with God in a "familiar walk" and an "intentional walk."

The Familiar Walk

Everyone walks with God in a particular, individual way. You could call it the "way things are" walk, the "just is" walk, or a familiar walk. Each person has a familiar walk; people can't help being who they are. As Christians we walk with God every moment of the day. God is with us when we wake up and when we go to sleep. At times we think prayers or think of Scripture. A brief conversation of talking and listening to God occurs. Dictionary.com primarily defines the word "familiar" as "Often encountered or seen. Having fair knowledge; acquainted. Of established friendship; intimate. Natural and unstudied; informal." Once someone is born again at the inner spiritual level, he or she is now on a Christian familiar walk. Listen to the picture in Romans 8:15-16:

> For you did not receive a spirit that makes you a slave again to fear, but you received the Spirit of sonship. And by him we cry, "Abba, Father." The Spirit himself testifies with our spirit that we are God's children.

This familiar walk is very important. It is through the power of

God displayed in the inner being (Ephesians 3:16-17) that lets you say no to temptations and yes to godliness. It is the familiar walk by which someone has the strength to be a martyr for Christ. It is by the familiar walk that people see in you the fruit of the Spirit. It is at this level that you surrender to God in a deeper relationship.

> Blessed is the man who does not walk in the counsel of the wicked or stand in the way of sinners or sit in the seat of mockers. But his delight is in the law of the LORD, and on his law he meditates day and night. (Psalm 1:1-2)

> Teach me your way, O LORD, and I will walk in your truth; give me an undivided heart, that I may fear your name. (Psalm 86:11)

> "...walk faithfully before me with all [your] heart and soul...." (1 Kings 2:4)

The Intentional Walk

The familiar walk is where real relationship takes place; however, the choices you make will substantially shape what your familiar walk will look like. You don't just become what you are—it happens in time. The familiar walk or "who we just are" walk needs guidance through focused time with God on a regular basis. An intentional walk—structured and consistent times of prayer and Bible reading—gives us strength and resilience in our familiar walk. These times of intentional interaction give energy and spark and renewal to a familiar walk. We refer to this focused or intentional time as home discipleship.

The intentional walk is more self-aware, more structured. Often at first, the discipline of an intentional walk feels like hard work or a legalistic chore; some Christians lean too heavily on their familiar walk with God and neglect the intentional or home-discipleship walk. However, when their familiar walk falters, they end up with nothing to fall back on, no habits and disciplines that keep them putting one foot in front of the other on their walk. It is like a married couple making a habit of a date night; it can feel artificial sometimes and perhaps it interrupts your schedule many weeks, but when tough times come and you continue that habit, it can see you through.

Neglecting an intentional walk has serious consequences. Many Christians have started to redefine a relationship with God in their own image: "God is what I want him to be instead of how he really is as revealed in Scripture." A familiar walk with God can drift. But an intentional or home-discipleship walk is supported by timeless Christian doctrines and creeds. This walk is supported by churches. Other Christians can check up on our intentional walk and keep us accountable. In home discipleship, we use patterns of Bible reading and prayer to lay the road for walking in a loving familiar walk with God. Many have called this discipleship time with God devotions.

> Teach them to your children, talking about them when you sit at home and when you walk along the road, when you lie down and when you get up. Write them on the doorframes of your houses and on your gates.... (Deuteronomy 11:19-20)

What is the essence of a devotional pattern? What actually goes on? When Pam and I took walks in our courtship, the basic elements of communication were the pattern of talking and listening repeatedly. When we relate to God, the key elements of talking and listening are also present.

Talking to God: Prayer

Talking to God is what Christians call prayer. Prayer can happen via our thoughts and our verbal words. Prayer can happen as we worship God with others. Prayer is simply communicating with God. The Bible talks a great deal about prayer; many Scripture passages are written-out prayers to God. Most of the Psalms are prayers to God, which became the songs of the Hebrew people. Prayer is more than a mere practice. Prayer is communicating to our God who hears us.

> The LORD is far from the wicked but he hears the prayer of the righteous. (Proverbs 15:29)

The pattern of repeated prayer is encouraged in the Bible. Colossians 4:2 says:

> Devote yourselves to prayer, being watchful and thankful.

Have you ever experienced an answered prayer? Maybe you experienced something beyond your ability to cope. You cried out to the Lord. He gave you the strength to deal with that day or that crisis. Maybe you prayed for direction. You were very confused as to what to do. You said, "Help me God!" and he did...big time. Maybe you received a "no" to one of your prayers, only later to find out that God saw something you did not see at that time. The fact is that when someone prays to God, God hears that prayer.

From the earliest pages of Scripture, we see the role of prayer in the life of a believer:

> Isaac prayed to the LORD on behalf of his wife, because she was barren. The LORD answered his prayer, and his wife Rebekah became pregnant. (Genesis 25:21)

The book of Psalms is really a book of prayers. In that book, we see some of the most passionate examples of prayer modeled. Many passages in Psalms encourage prayer:

> Therefore let everyone who is godly pray to you while you may be found; surely when the mighty waters rise, they will not reach

him. (Psalm 32:6)

If a believer cries out to the Lord, his or her very words will be heard. God will be involved in your future. God is not some Santa Claus in the sky; when we ask something of God in prayer, we get three types of answers. Those answers will be "yes," "no," or "wait." These are very similar to the answers children get when they ask their earthly father or mother a question.

Prayer often takes on the form of worship. We may cry out to the Lord in praise and adoration in a worship setting.

> "It is written," [Jesus] said to them, "'My house will be a house of prayer'; but you have made it 'a den of robbers.'" (Luke 19:46)

Prayer engages your heart and mind to express your praise, confessions, requests, and intercessions to God. Prayers can be written down; they can be thought, verbalized, memorized; they can be sung or cried out. You don't have to be a prayer expert to pray. The key thing is that you talk to God.

Listening to God: Bible Reading

Listening to God happens primarily through reading and meditating on God's Word. The Bible not only is the number-one bestselling book of all time, it is the infallible, inerrant Word that God speaks to humans.

God may choose to speak to us in many ways in our familiar walk: through the counsel of a friend, through a Christian book or song, through the beauty of his creation. He has spoken to people directly and indirectly in many ways throughout history. But in each case, we should be careful to check what we are hearing against the teachings of the Word of God. The Bible says that Satan masquerades as an angel of light. In an intentional walk—the habitual, day-in and day-out pattern of listening to

God—we use the Bible as a consistent, reliable source of hearing God's message for us.

Sometimes it might seem like a Bible passage does not have much to say to us. We might get the itch for a more directly applicable counseling session or theological book. But in the Old Testament book of Isaiah, God promises that exposure to his words will bring life:

> As the rain and the snow come down from heaven, and do not return to it without watering the earth and making it bud and flourish, so that it yields seed for the sower and bread for the eater, so is my word that goes out from my mouth: It will not return to me empty, but will accomplish what I desire and achieve the purpose for which I sent it. (Isaiah 55:10-11)

The Bible does not always comfort us; sometimes it lays us bare and gives us correction that our best friend or our Christian magazine might never confront us with:

> For the word of God is living and active. Sharper than any double-edged sword, it penetrates even to dividing soul and spirit, joints and marrow; it judges the thoughts and attitudes of the heart. Nothing in all creation is hidden from God's sight. Everything is uncovered and laid bare before the eyes of him to whom we must give account. (Hebrews 4:12-13)

Listening to God can happen whenever you open your Bible during daily devotions, couples devotions, or family devotions. The pattern of listening to his voice can happen at a Bible study or in hearing a sermon. God speaks through his Word, and you and I grow in our relationship as we open our hearts and listen to what God is telling us. Ephesians 6:17b tells us to take "the sword of the Spirit, which is the word of God." A vital relationship with God will be a relationship that is full of the Word of God!

Repeatedly: Creating a Habit

If Pam and I had decided to take only one walk, we would not be married today. A talking-and-listening pattern has to recur repeatedly if relationships are to deepen. The walks were not optional. Those walks made a big difference. Walking with God is no different. We need to walk with God over and over again. The Bible calls on us to seek the Lord while he is near:

> Seek the LORD while he may be found; call on him while he is near. Let the wicked forsake his way and the evil man his thoughts. Let him turn to the LORD, and he will have mercy on him, and to our God, for he will freely pardon. (Isaiah 55:6-7)

There is an incredible story in the Bible of a man named Enoch. This man walked with the Lord so closely that one day the Lord took him off this earth. Genesis 5:24 says:

> Enoch walked with God; then he was no more, because God took him away.

Enoch is mentioned again in the New Testament book of Hebrews:

> By faith Enoch was taken from this life, so that he did not experience death; he could not be found, because God had taken him away. For before he was taken, he was commended as one who pleased God. (Hebrews 11:5)

Walking with God repeatedly is a challenging endeavor in our modern world. We have to be intentional about actually doing it, or most times it will not happen.

If Christianity is going to spread spontaneously, talking and listening repeatedly to God must be front and center once again. Either we are connected to God or we are not. If you and I really have a spiritual dream that we want to see come true, it is going to take finding a way to walk with God.

79

Talking and listening repeatedly to God is not just a devotional pattern. Talking and listening repeatedly to God is the timeless path that every believer walks. It is the path where life transformation occurs. It is the path where you grow closer to God and his power is displayed more and more in your life. This is the path where the wind of the Holy Spirit blows on us as we talk and listen to God repeatedly.

The Windy Path

There is much debate over how a person is drawn into a relationship with God. We know it is by grace through faith. It is a gift of God. How is it that this gift of relationship is taken to heart by some and not by others? Some theologians will argue election. Some will argue free will. While I believe that somehow God picked me as his child, I am not some robot programmed to be saved. There is an element of mystery, kind of like "the way of a man with a maiden." I agree with that old hymn, "I Know Not Why God's Wondrous Grace," which says, "I know not why God's wondrous grace to me he hath made known, nor why, unworthy, Christ in love redeemed me for his own." The chorus of the song quotes 2 Timothy 1:12b:

> ...because I know whom I have believed, and am convinced that
> he is able to guard what I have entrusted to him for that day.

Here is an interesting question: How does God's grace of a relationship get to us? Which person of the Trinity quickens our hearts to establish and grow into a relationship with God? The Bible teaches that the Holy Spirit comes upon believers to connect them with God in a relationship. Notice this example of the apostle Peter preaching while the Holy Spirit was poured out:

> While Peter was still speaking these words, the Holy Spirit came

on all who heard the message. The circumcised believers who had come with Peter were astonished that the gift of the Holy Spirit had been poured out even on the Gentiles. (Acts 10:44-45)

We notice in Scripture that God's grace somehow gets to us through the work of the Holy Spirit. I love the example of that found in John. John 3:16 is one of the most famous gospel passages. Jesus is talking to Nicodemus at night about the subject of being born again in a spiritual sense. Most of us have heard:

For God so loved the world that he gave his one and only Son, that whoever believes in him shall not perish but have eternal life. (John 3:16)

It is interesting to note a few comments Jesus gives to Nicodemus earlier in the conversation. These comments illustrate some of the mystery of a relationship with God:

"Flesh gives birth to flesh, but the Spirit gives birth to spirit. You should not be surprised at my saying, 'You must be born again.' The wind blows wherever it pleases. You hear its sound, but you cannot tell where it comes from or where it is going. So it is with everyone born of the Spirit." "How can this be?" Nicodemus asked. (John 3:6-9)

What can be concluded about someone who comes to God? How do you continue to grow spiritually? You and I need to find the spiritually windy path and stay there.

Let's say a person who had never felt wind asked me to bring him to a place where there was wind. Since I live near Chicago, the "windy city," maybe I would bring him downtown. Or since I live in the country, I might bring him to my house. If there is wind to be had, we usually get it where we live. There are places that do not get wind that much. If you stay in the house, you may feel just a draft. Can I guarantee that wind will happen at my house? No. But each of us knows more or less where we are apt to find wind and where we are not.

That is how it is with a relationship with God. There are places that are windy, so to speak, and places that are still. While God can change a heart anywhere, God ordinarily does not blow his wind in wicked places. On the other hand, there are places or life practices that let you "feel" lots of wind. And those windy places are usually associated with the Bible and with prayer. I'll give you some examples:

- A person who reads the Bible and prays on a daily basis has placed himself or herself in a windy place with God.
- A couple who read the Bible together and prays together will be refreshed by God's breeze.
- A family that pauses every day to read the Bible and pray will be inviting the wind of the Spirit.
- A group of like-minded believers gathering in a setting where God's Word is read and prayers are spoken will bathe in God's warm airstream.
- A group of worshippers who open the Word together, who corporately pray and praise God together are at a place where mighty wind often blows.
- When Christian leaders or pastors get together and open the Word of God and pray for the work of the kingdom, strong holds of the evil one are blown down.
- When someone who does not know God dares to read the Bible and dares to talk to God with a repentant heart, the separation of sin and Satan are toppled over with a hurricane from the Holy Spirit.

What do all these examples have in common? They all involve God's Word and prayer. A relationship with God is a mystery, to be sure, but we can more or less determine where the wind of the Spirit is likely to be blowing. We cannot guarantee to catch the wind, but we know that if we stick around long enough we are likely to feel it. It is our choice to stay where we are or to pursue a path where God's power will be blowing.

It is important to keep in mind the pursuit of God's Spirit; without it, talking and listening to God repeatedly can easily become routine and dull or an empty exercise in which we take pride. The Pharisees read the Scripture a lot and they prayed a lot. But they were competitors of God. They practiced their faith, but their heart had little actual love for God. They had a form of godliness but denied its power. While hypocrisy and pride are possibilities even today, it's no excuse to avoid the practices of Bible reading and prayer. There is just no way to have a vital relationship without talking and listening to God repeatedly. The fact is that God's Word does not return empty if your heart is open to receive it. The fact is that God hears your prayers as you learn to depend on him as your source of life. A vital walk with God is a very important part of your discipleship. Jesus spent time with his disciples and taught them to be his instruments to spread the gospel. When you spend time with God and walk with him, you are being "discipled" to be his instruments to spread Christianity all over this world.

Thinking Reproducibility

I'll never forget eavesdropping once at a restaurant. I had just completed two days of seminars on reproducible evangelism and discipleship. I was eating breakfast with my brother John when a man and a woman were seated next to us. The man was very loud, and I could hear everything they said. The conversation went something like this:

"Sandy, glad you agreed to be taught what it means to be a Christian," said Bob.

"Thank you, I don't know much about Christianity, but I now

believe in Jesus and I want to be a Christian," Sandy confessed.

I decided to completely eavesdrop on this conversation. I told my brother quietly, "Let's listen and hear how Bob will be able to reproduce Christianity to Sandy." What we heard was a complicated depiction of Christianity. Bob began by explaining that now that Sandy was a Christian she would need to be aware of many important things. Bob started with the rapture. He talked about different theories of the second coming of Christ. He then told her how she should believe.

Next Bob talked about his quiet time. He mentioned that he gets up at 4:00 a.m. and studies the Bible for an hour. Then he meditates and prays for another hour. She was going to have to learn to do this now that she was a Christian. He continued his description of Christianity for the next hour. He used the word "if" often. When asked about movies and drinking, he went on a long and detailed criticism of everything that comes out of Hollywood. He then went on to say that people who smoke and drink have serious spiritual problems.

I noticed her reaction to his presentation. At first her countenance was bright and interested. She asked a few questions. Bob over-answered her questions. Soon she stopped asking questions. Her arms crossed, and her face no longer looked interested in Bob's lengthy explanations. He concluded his meeting by saying, "If you want to be a fruitful Christian, you'll need to know these kinds of things. I am willing to meet with you every week to disciple you." At this point, the conversation came to an abrupt halt. Sandy put some cash on the table to pay for the meal. Bob refused to let her pay. "Put that money back in your purse," he said. Bob asked Sandy when they wanted to meet again. Sandy said wearily, "Bob, thank you for meeting with me; if I am interested to hear more, I'll call you." She quickly rose to her feet and exited. Bob paid the bill and left.

For his part, Bob was just trying to reproduce Christianity as he knew it. He was spiritually reached and nurtured at a specific church with specific spiritual emphases. The dynamic of his walk was shaped by that background. When he tried to reproduce his faith, he was trying to share many levels of spiritual content.

Christianity as a whole has many facets to it. As a movement, Christianity has 2,000 years of history and doctrines. Some of these doctrines have been debated for generations. Does anybody really know how many angels can balance on the head of a pin? Christianity has various denominations, each of them with their own doctrinal peculiarities. Christianity is a cultural way of life for a lot of people. For many, the sum total of Christianity is the church they are attending right now. There is a variety of styles of approaching God used by the various Christian churches; different churches have different emphases. In other words, different churches have different understandings of what a windy path looks like.

Some churches believe that knowledge is the key emphasis, that the most windy place of all is the knowledge path. I understand this one because I was raised in a conservative Christian Reformed home. Even though my dad was a mechanic and my mom was a factory worker, we talked about fine points of doctrine in our home. When I became a young adult and was ready to publicly profess my faith, I appeared before the elders of my local church. My elders were very concerned about what I knew. Yes, they were interested in my profession of Jesus as my Savior and Lord, but they wanted to make sure I knew what atonement meant. They asked me questions about topics like sanctification and justification. Did I know the Reformation understanding of the doctrine of T.U.L.I.P. (which I will not even try to define for you now)? The leaders in our church felt that the windiest place, the place where the Holy Spirit reaches us most powerfully, is a mind that retains proper spiritual knowledge.

Other churches will claim that commitment is the windiest path. In churches like this, the worship service is often set up as an event that prompts a commitment to Christ. The message and music aim at convicting the heart and spurring on repentance. The evangelist Billy Graham's service is a good example of this: There is music, there are testimonies, there is the message, and the conclusion is the altar call. Commitment is the climate of the event. For many churches, this is their windiest path.

Other churches will desire to create an experience. When people "feel" the closeness of God in a worship experience, they feel the wind. Often Pentecostal churches have this emphasis. Often mega-churches have similar approaches. They design their worship service for a relevant experience. The topics are about practical issues like parenting and marriage. The worshippers are often asked to just sit back and enjoy the experience.

Other churches center on liturgy—repeated, predictable patterns that are practiced at every service. Catholic or Anglican churches are good examples of liturgical churches. As you weekly walk through the prayers and a message that often conforms to the church year, you connect with history, with spiritual rhythm, with other churches in your denomination. Liturgy is a stable, grounding force that develops meaning as the habits are practiced over an entire lifetime.

Of course, these categories are an oversimplification; the boundaries between these camps are not as rigid as the descriptions may suggest. It is too simplistic to say that liturgical churches are not interested in knowledge. Or that commitment churches are not interested in experience. Knowledge, commitment, experience, and liturgy find their way into every church or denominational path. Some churches have power combinations of two or more of these values. I am illustrating that there are a lot of complicating factors in reproducing Christianity. Liturgy in itself is not relationship with God. Knowledge in itself is not relationship with God. Commitment in itself is not relationship with God. Experience in itself is not relationship with God. They are all important ingredients, but a relationship cannot be reduced to one of these ingredients.

These four words—knowledge, commitment, experience, and liturgy—are relational factors. They are all key ingredients of a relationship. These factors are important in human relationships too. I needed to "know" a lot about Pam, and she needed to know a lot about me. We needed the liturgy of courtship, going through the time-honored traditions of going on dates, buying flowers, etc. We experienced all the feelings of love and tenderness and connection together as we grew in relationship. Eventually we made a commitment to marry each other. There is no way to take out any one of those elements and still have our relationship work. Reducing Christianity to learning doctrine, praying the sinner's prayer, feeling the Holy Spirit, or attending church will just not work. It is a relationship—a relationship fed by the simple practice of talking and listening repeatedly.

Let's return to our friends Bob and Sandy. Bob was trying to reproduce Christianity as he knew it, a very complicated Christianity. I believe that Bob would have been hard pressed to simply express the heart of Christianity. He was unclear as to the essentials of Christianity.

Sandy was a new believer. I heard her say that she had just made a commitment to Christ at Bob's church. She checked a box indicating that she wanted to know more about Christianity. Bob must have called her to set up an appointment. Sandy came into the meeting with a series of practical questions such as: How do I succeed at praying or reading the Bible? She had a few curiosity questions like: Are Christians allowed to see movies? What does the Bible say about drinking?

Sandy left with a sense of heaviness. The conversation with

Bob raised questions that she dared not ask. She was afraid that the answers would disqualify her as a Christian. She likely concluded that she had better take this Christian thing very slowly.

So what does a reproducible Christianity look like? Reproducible Christianity starts with a keen sense of what it is you are trying to reproduce. At the very heart of the matter, when you and I share Christianity, we are introducing someone else to a relationship with God. The kind of church you attend, the songs you sing, the type of study Bible you use, your views of smoking and drinking, what time you wake up for devotions— these are all secondary things that go along with Christianity but are not its core. We have to be very careful that we share something that starts a person toward a healthy spiritual future.

Reproducing a relationship is not so simple. A relationship is somewhat hard to quantify. I have given the gospel again and again to people. For some they just do not see it. For others they not only get it, but they want to take that next step in a walk with God. I can't reproduce my many experiences, my trials and defeats. I can't recreate apt words that have been spoken to me when I had big decisions to make. I can't reproduce in someone else's life the times when God showed up in mine just when I needed him.

There are, however, some things I can reproduce. I can reproduce relational patterns or habits that are simple and easy to maintain. I can reproduce a walk. This walk will include prayer (talking to God) and Bible reading (listening to God) repeatedly. It will involve talking and listening to God within the key connections of your life: your personal life, your marriage, your family, your like-minded friends or small groups, your churches, your broader kingdom of God associations, and your evangelistic contacts. A walk with God within the context of your seven connections is what I mean when I say "home discipleship." Discipleship is the process of growing (sanctification) in a relationship with God and helping others to do the same. It starts in the home (your personal life, marriage, and family) because that is where you have the greatest influence and greatest accountability.

Intentionality in Home Discipleship

Home discipleship is not home schooling, but the similarity is to be noted. Home schooling is a movement that has spread throughout the United States and Canada where a parent (usually the mother) leads the patterns and habits of education in the home. The home-schooling movement has shown how effective the home can be as a learning environment. In fact, if you home school, you may already have many of the habits and disciplines that fit well with home discipleship.

My wife and I started home schooling in 1994. One of the first things we realized is how hard it was to get the family on one page with one goal. My wife and I were driven by the fact that it was our responsibility to make sure the children learned something. My wife ordered a home-school curriculum, and she set up a schedule. New, good habits of learning were established. The television was limited. The computer was put in its place. At that time, we were in the practice of reading the Bible and praying in our personal lives, our marriage, and our family, but it was difficult to stay consistent. After we starting home schooling, we were able to benefit from the good habits that were formed in home schooling. Home schooling really woke us up to the role of the family in connecting our lives to God.

You must be very intentional in your habits if you want to succeed in home schooling. School does not happen automatically. There must be a specific curriculum. There must be a starting time. There must be engagement into a set of materials. Home schooling just doesn't happen without specific efforts. Even the home-schooling movement of un-schooling is filled with intentional patterns.

We live in a time in history when you and I must be intentional in home-discipleship practices as well. Only a generation ago most families would observe a dinner hour. Christian families would tie their Bible reading and prayer to that daily habit. Today the expectation is that children are doing extracurricular activities many evenings instead of eating dinner with the family. Often when a family does sit down together, it is in front of the television. The loss of a dinner hour means the loss of a habit to tie Bible reading and prayer to. If you want to start habits of family devotional time in your home, you will have to make a conscious decision to be different from the American culture around you. You will have to say that the home is a priority. Instead of sacrificing a home life in the name of the kids' social life (going out to movies, instant messaging friends) or skill enrichment (a full plate of sports, arts, and activities), you must come to the conclusion that a connection to their parents and siblings and God will serve them well. Even a great youth program or Sunday school at your church is no substitute for time spent reading the Bible together and praying as a family. Youth pastors come and go, but as a parent and a family, you are there for each other for a lifetime.

In the late 1990s I helped conduct a poll at five typical Christian schools. The question was simple: "Is the Bible read in your home with any regularity?" We found that only twelve percent of the students said that the Bible was habitually read in the home. The fact is that most Christian homes do not read the Bible on a regular basis. Several years ago, a large mega-church in Houston contacted me to help increase Bible reading in their church. The discipleship pastor told of a poll he conducted with individuals and families of the church. He found out that the Bible-reading practice of his church was less than ten percent. His goal was to double Bible reading. He thought it was going to be unrealistic to go beyond that.

Complicating the whole matter is the ailing state of the family in our society. Today more and more fathers have checked out of their responsibility to lead their homes. Many fathers are more interested in sports than they are in gathering their family for devotions. Many fathers have become so busy that they themselves have little time to develop their own walks with God. I have noticed, hanging around the home-schooling culture for many years, that often the father has stopped leading the home-discipleship effort and that the wife is responsible for any discipleship that happens in a home.

Mothers in our society are also suffering. Often mothers are working. Mothers are torn with being responsible for child rearing and sustaining a career. The mothers who do stay at home are busy chauffeuring their children to a whole host of activities. Often home-school mothers are doing everything alone.

This is all complicated by the large amount of estranged families. Children are with Dad one weekend; they are with Mom the next. Most of us desire a vital walk with God, but our whole life situation holds us back.

The point is: If you want to actually do home discipleship, you are going to have to go against the grain in our technological and fragmented culture. If you want to actually walk with God, you have to be intentional and focused to find time, very practically, to read the Bible and pray. Therefore, when reproducing Christianity, you also have to reproduce intentionality. The remainder of this book will be filled with practical steps toward making Bible reading and prayer intentional in each of your seven connections.

A Culture of Home Discipleship

If intentionality is one key toward reproducibility, the other key is cultural reinforcement. "Culture" is a popular word today in businesses and churches; it is a way of describing the habits and practices of those who share common values. For instance, a business may want to have a corporate culture that puts the customer first. They set up their business practices around customer service. They invent phrases like, "The customer is always right." The same thing has happened in churches. Some churches have a "seeker" corporate culture. Some churches have a hospitality corporate culture. The habits and the practices of the staff and leadership team enhance corporate values and vision. It is positive peer pressure. This culture is noticeable. It is distinctive. It reinforces the values of the corporate identity.

The same is true about home discipleship as well. If you desire to walk with God during your lifetime, the culture of your life will be countercultural to the way of the broader culture. You'll still be in the world. You'll live here. You'll work here. You'll learn things here. You'll be a lot like Daniel and his friends who were stuck in Babylon.

> To these four young men God gave knowledge and understanding of all kinds of literature and learning. And Daniel could understand visions and dreams of all kinds. At the end of the time set by the king to bring them in, the chief official presented them to Nebuchadnezzar. The king talked with them, and he found none equal to Daniel, Hananiah, Mishael and Azariah; so they entered the king's service. In every matter of wisdom and understanding about which the king questioned them, he found them ten times better than all the magicians and enchanters in his whole kingdom. (Daniel 1:17-20)

Throughout the book of Daniel, it is very clear that Daniel, Hananiah, Mishael, and Azariah had a different culture operating at a spiritual level. They had a walking-with-God culture. At times that spiritual culture was challenged, but that culture was Daniel's and his friends' real identity. That was illustrated so well late in Daniel's life. Daniel had enemies because he would not take bribes. Daniel did his work with honesty and integrity. Many corrupt officials hated Daniel for this. They noticed that Daniel had a culture of daily prayer to his God. They invented a scheme by which the cultural clash of Daniel's prayer life would come into lethal conflict with the broader cultural practice of emperor worship that was so prevalent in that time. So the corrupt officials said to King Darius:

> "O King Darius, live forever! The royal administrators, prefects, satraps, advisers and governors have all agreed that the king should issue an edict and enforce the decree that anyone who prays to any god or man during the next thirty days, except to you, O king, shall be thrown into the lions' den." (Daniel 6:6a-7)

The king agreed. Daniel had an intentional home-discipleship practice of praying three times a day. The corrupt officials thought they had him. They went to the king:

> "Daniel, who is one of the exiles from Judah, pays no attention to you, O king, or to the decree you put in writing. He still prays three times a day." (Daniel 6:13)

Daniel was thrown into the lion's den. But God rescued Daniel. Daniel's home-discipleship culture was his way of life. God is God, and he is to be worshiped every day. God was glorified in the life of Daniel. Though Daniel and his friends were in this world, they were not of this world. They lived for God. God-walking culture was their culture.

God-walking culture must be our culture. The habits and practices of our life all lead to one pursuit: to walk with God both now and in all eternity. We are to share these home-discipleship habits and practices with our children.

Walk in all the way that the LORD your God has commanded you,

93

so that you may live and prosper and prolong your days in the land that you will possess. (Deuteronomy 5:33)

These commandments that I give you today are to be upon your hearts. Impress them on your children. Talk about them when you sit at home and when you walk along the road, when you lie down and when you get up. Tie them as symbols on your hands and bind them on your foreheads. Write them on the doorframes of your houses and on your gates. (Deuteronomy 6:6-9)

The fact is that you and I cannot succeed at anything without immersing ourselves in a culture. If you want to learn to play the guitar, you take lessons, you buy books, you spend time with others who play the guitar, you listen to music, you find TV programs about great guitar players. Success is not just the technical aspect of arranging your fingers in the right way and learning to strum in rhythm; success is being inspired, excited, connected, informed, and dreaming big dreams with what you can do with music.

In the same way, the Christian walk isn't about logging a certain number of minutes each day praying or reading the Bible. It's about sharing it with other people, bouncing ideas off your pastor, involving a neighbor in conversation, reading up on what other people in the kingdom are doing. It's walking the walk and sharing the walk. The rest of this book will be about how you can make a walk with God reach every significant human connection you have—how you can create a culture around you that supports you and your family in this wonderful journey with God. As you do this, your Christian influence will spontaneously spread.

Sharing our walk with God—discipleship—is the central command in the great commission. Just before Jesus ascended into heaven after his resurrection from the dead, he told his disciples that the good news of a relationship with God was to be shared unto the ends of the earth:

> "Therefore go and make disciples of all nations, baptizing them in the name of the Father and of the Son and of the Holy Spirit, and teaching them to obey everything I have commanded you. And surely I am with you always, to the very end of the age." (Matthew 28:19-20)

Jesus didn't say to teach doctrine to all nations, to create spiritual experiences, or to pedal commitment cards to all nations. He asked us to disciple all nations, to share with them and help them develop a walk with God. A walk where God's agenda is our agenda. A walk where we love the Lord our God with all our heart and our neighbor as ourselves. A walk that intentionally works in our day. A walk with God we can do with our families. A walk where our familiarity with God and his ways transforms our lives. A walk that can be reproduced. A walk that was established out of grace. A home-discipleship walk that affects every relationship in our lives. A walk where others see our culture of relating to God and we learn to share it with those around us.

Chapter 5

Connection One: A Personal Walk

CHERYL WAS born in a home that didn't honor God. Her '60s-generation parents believed that religion was harmful for the human animal. Her parents believed that ultimate goodness was to exercise freedom in a way that did not harm others. She was nurtured in the humanism walk. Her parents' spiritual dream was to help others realize their human freedom. She saw her parents have inappropriate relationships with other couples. She saw the drugs and alcohol fueling her parents' walk of despair. The crashes after the parties and orgies were hard for a little girl to take. But this was the only path she knew.

By the time she was in high school, Cheryl was following the path of her parents. She was sexually active by age 14; her parents supplied her with contraceptives. She graduated from high school with good grades and went to a respected college. She found a group of students to hang around with who had the same walk. She lived wild. She partied. She graduated. She moved in with her boyfriend. They partied. They had very humanistic views of sexuality. She held a good job to support her lifestyle.

Something was missing from her life. In fact, she was secretly miserable and contemplating suicide. Fortunately, she became friends at work with someone who was very different from her. Sandy had a walk with God. At first, Cheryl would attack Sandy and talk behind her back. Sandy was hurt by the treatment but returned it with compassion not contempt. Cheryl was looking for Sandy's weaknesses. She found some. Sometimes Sandy worried about her health and other things. But Cheryl worried about everything. Overall, Sandy was different. She seemed to have a peace and joy about her. She was genuine. Sandy would read her Bible at break and say a little prayer before they ate. Cheryl noticed it more than she would admit. When the boss treated all the women in the department in an abusive way, Sandy would forgive him and move on. Cheryl hated the boss more each time and tried to defeat his control by flirting with him and trying to sleep with him. This brought no joy to Cheryl.

One day Cheryl hit the wall, literally. Her car slammed into a railing. She was barely alive. There was doubt whether she was going to live. She survived, but it was going to be a long haul in the hospital. Her boyfriend visited but did not stay long. Her parents visited but did not know what to say or do. Her friend Sandy visited and asked Cheryl if she could read the Bible and pray for her. Cheryl was too distraught to refuse a friend. Over the month in the hospital, her parents occasionally came but did not say long. Her boyfriend announced that he was moving out and that he was moving in with Jessica. Cheryl understood. *No commitment* was the mantra of their lifestyle. Cheryl cried. Her former boyfriend left.

Sandy came often. She read the Bible often. She prayed often. Cheryl started to dream that she was a Christian. She looked forward to hearing the Bible read. When Sandy prayed, Cheryl started to copy Sandy and close her eyes, too. She asked if Sandy would let her borrow her Bible. Sandy handed it to her and showed her a few basics. She told her to start with the book of John. Cheryl read. She asked questions of Sandy. And Cheryl also prayed simple prayers. Most of her prayers were for practical things, like "Lord, don't let me be ugly after my injuries heal!" Some of her prayers were dealing with her sinful lifestyle: "Lord, forgive me for living the way I was."

Sandy brought her pastor once. Cheryl had a lot of questions for him. *Why would God let this happen to me? Will God forgive me for what I have done?* She listened to God by reading about forgiveness and new life. She started to dream about a relationship with God.

One evening late in the night, Cheryl prayed for Christ to accept her as his child. The heaviness didn't leave her all at once. At times she doubted if anything had happened but noticed that her interest in hearing the voice of God in Scripture increased. Her prayers were becoming more and more frequent. She asked Sandy to bring her to church.

God certainly had mercy on Cheryl. She left the hospital no worse off physically than when she entered. But she was very different. Her old boyfriend was delighted to she how pretty she still was. He complimented her looks and invited her to his place with Jessica. She went. They drank. They flirted. She succumbed to temptation. She woke up miserable. All day long, her conscience was talking to her. She remembered words she read in Scripture. She asked God to forgive her many times that day. In tears, she confessed everything to Sandy. Sandy told her that she was now walking with God and that God was actually speaking to her and that she was talking to God. Sandy led her in a prayer of confession, and Cheryl asked Jesus to be her Lord and Savior.

Now Cheryl has been walking with God for many years. She is now familiar with Christ. She reads the Bible and prays often. She attends church and has led others to the Lord. She isn't perfect, but she has been made perfect. She married a vital Christian man. She and Sandy are still close friends.

What happened in Cheryl's life? She formed a relationship walk with the God of the universe. This walk changed her life. Her personal connection with God was powerful enough to actually transform her lifestyle and choices. She has new friends and new hope.

Familiar and Intentional Walks

Every person has a familiar walk and an intentional walk. The key question is, with whom are you walking? Cheryl was born into a family that had a secular spiritual dream. The familiar walk in her family was one of hedonism. Cheryl's parents' spiritual dream was to be one with pleasure. Their dream was to worship at the feet of Aphrodite, the goddess of love. They surrendered their will. They also dreamed to share this with Cheryl. Her parents modeled the culture of pleasure to her. She was familiar with that walk and familiar with the humanism god.

Cheryl and her family had an intentional walk, too. These were practical habits that gave the "hooks" to keep Cheryl's family supported. Her parents studied humanistic writings. They were seriously influenced by evolutionism. They were subscribers to pornographic materials and media outlets. They intentionally sought drugs and other narcotics. They were not afraid to intentionally support Cheryl to become who they were by helping her use contraceptives even at a young age.

Her humanism walk included the familiar and the intentional. Both worked together to support a life worshipping idols. The fact is that humans are religious beings at the core. The apostle Paul acknowledged that in Athens:

Paul then stood up in the meeting of the Areopagus and said:

"Men of Athens! I see that in every way you are very religious. For as I walked around and looked carefully at your objects of worship, I even found an altar with this inscription: TO AN UNKNOWN GOD. Now what you worship as something unknown I am going to proclaim to you. The God who made the world and everything in it is the Lord of heaven and earth and does not live in temples built by hands." (Acts 17:22-24)

The Athenians had a familiar and intentional walk with many gods. They had group meetings and altars that brought them intentionally to their idols. They had a familiar walk with their gods as well, an expression of a spiritual dream to attain wisdom and favor. But Paul graciously and intentionally introduced them to the God of the universe. Some who heard did not receive the gospel and continued in their walk of idolatry. Some started to walk with God, and Paul was called to lead them on the walk of life. The Word of God does not return void.

A few men became followers of Paul and believed. Among them was Dionysius, a member of the Areopagus, also a woman named Damaris, and a number of others. (Acts 17:34)

Let's return to Cheryl's story. Cheryl had a friend named Sandy who was walking with God. Cheryl did not notice the intentional things that supported Sandy's walk at first. What Cheryl noticed about Sandy was her familiar walk. Sandy actually liked her life. She was at peace. She was forgiving and generous. She actually knew how to love unconditionally. Whereas Cheryl was contemplating suicide, Sandy was content and found life filled with meaning and opportunity. Cheryl also noticed that Sandy had problems just like her. But she reacted differently to problems and stress. It was the familiar walk that Cheryl saw at first.

When a crisis occurred, it was the familiar walk of Sandy's unconditional love that compelled Cheryl to listen to the Word of

God proclaimed. So Sandy started to read the Bible and pray. The Word of God cut to Cheryl's very heart. Inside of Cheryl, the final battle of a spiritual war was raging. The intentional activities of opening the Word of God and praying were happening. Listening to God and talking to God were now being pursued. And the wind was blowing. It wasn't that long before Cheryl started to walk with God. And even if there were rocky moments at the start, her walk with God would grow stronger as she continued her intentional walking alongside leaders like Sandy, other believers, and the church.

Home-Discipleship Prayer

When Christianity spontaneously spreads, it happens because individuals really have a walk with God. These people tend and nourish their personal connection to God. They practice the Christian faith not out of family tradition or social convention or a need to feel righteous, but out of an overflowing love for Jesus and a desire to be like him. It is relatively easy to hide a poor personal connection to God in many churches; few will ask if you have a consistent prayer life or Bible-reading habit. But God knows you, and you are completely naked before him. You can hide your heart from other people but not from God. Do you feel abundant and joyful in your walk with God or reluctant and weary? God desires your whole self, not half-measures. It is not enough to get by, gleaning pieces of others' spiritual walks through sermons and songs and calling it your own. It is only through a vital, growing relationship with God that others will sense that vitality and desire to know God as well.

Let us first start with the habit of prayer. What is your pattern of talking to God? How often do you pray? Prayer might be a line of praise to God as we are driving down the street or it might involve time set aside to follow a formal prayer guide.

102

Familiar prayer patterns and intentional prayer patterns are both very important in talking with God.

Home-discipleship prayer is an intentional, scheduled time of talking to God. It usually occurs in the practice of a daily devotional time. Many people write down or journal their prayers. Some follow prayer guides such as the Book of Common Prayer. Reading the book of Psalms regularly puts you in touch with beautiful prayers that you can make your own. A good prayer tool is the ACTS guide. ACTS stands for *adoration, confession, thanksgiving,* and *supplication,* four elements of prayer taken from the Lord's Prayer that Jesus taught to his disciples:

> "This, then, is how you should pray:
> "'Our Father in heaven, hallowed be your name, (*Adoration*)
> Your kingdom come, your will be done on earth as it is in heaven.
> Give us today our daily bread. (*Supplication*)
> Forgive us our debts, as we also have forgiven our debtors.
> (*Confession*)
> And lead us not into temptation, but deliver us from the evil one.
> For yours is the kingdom and the power and the glory forever.
> (*Thanksgiving*)
> Amen.'" (Matthew 6:9-13)

The ACTS guide is a way of helping you organize your daily prayers. I found it helpful to create ACTS sheets to jot down my prayers, so that I could review them later and see how God was answering my prayers. I printed up notepads with the words "Adoration, Confession, Thanksgiving, Supplication" on them so that I could share them with others. You can create your own and keep them in a notebook if you find this guide useful.

At one point, church planter Steve Elzinga and I put together a "Connection Planner" that placed prayer at the center of your day. We had been trying to help people find daily time to fit prayer into their schedule, but the Lord seemed to show us:

Prayer is not merely an item on our "to do" list, but the "to do" list itself is full of the things that we need to bring to God in prayer. We learned that instead of fitting God into our schedule, we fit our schedule into our relationship with God. Our daily planners designated the scheduling area as the "Prayer/To Do List." The Connection Planner also encouraged people to pray through the seven connections and to read the Bible each day. You can make your own planner like this or see Appendix B to learn how to purchase similar planners.

Another type of prayer to God is the "while you are living" or familiar prayer. Since our minds and hearts are able to flit between human encounters and divine encounters, a person can spend a good part of the day aware of God's presence and informally talking to him. I can be riding in the car, when suddenly I "think" a prayer. Suddenly, I'm talking to God about something. Maybe something or someone is troubling me. I open up my heart to God wherever I am. This is an example of God's presence in our lives and how intimate that can be. This type of prayerful communion can occur as you sing or listen to a song in worship. Suddenly, you are speaking to God with groans or praise that words cannot express.

Familiar prayer might sometimes feel more honest and real than intentional prayer. But if you depend on familiar prayer alone, you will gradually lose creativity and passion in your familiar prayers. Intentional prayer supports and encourages the spontaneous prayers. Again, marriage is a good parallel: Much of the marriage talking is familiar. You talk about the kids; you talk about the clogged sewer that needs to be fixed. In familiar talking, you'll even communicate an "I love you." But if the familiar talking is all that is done, you miss out on going to the next level. In marriage there are greater levels of communicating available to you—spiritual, emotional, and physical. You have to make an intentional effort to go deeper; you have to schedule time to talk instead of just talking whenever the urge strikes you. Without the scheduled talking, it can be easy to drift apart, and the urge to talk will diminish. The same happens with prayer: Without a regular habit of turning to God for an extended time, the chances diminish that we will turn to him in familiar prayers throughout our day. I am not meaning to criticize a familiar prayer life. I just know that you and I can overuse spontaneous prayer. We need to have a balanced prayer walk.

Home-Discipleship Bible Reading

I counted them: The Reyenga family has at least forty-five Bibles in our home. With that many Bibles, I may have even missed some. I have hundreds of books that quote Bible passages. I have a large number of Bible commentaries. I studied Old Testament Hebrew and know New Testament Greek. I am committed to practicing home discipleship in my personal life. I love reading the Bible and praying. I love listening and talking to God repeatedly. I love walking with God each day. I have a spiritual dream of being close to God. I notice a difference when I neglect to open the Bible and pray in my personal life. I feel less effective in everything. I am convinced that walking with God is very important!

However, I find that sometimes I struggle to find a Bible when I am ready to practice home discipleship in my personal life. How is it possible that I can't find one of the forty-five Bibles in the house? I relate to the God of the universe, who wants to connect to me personally, but somehow I can get sidetracked by a newspaper, a phone call, a kid call, or some crisis. And then, so often, I never find my way back to God that day.

The fact is that a discipleship walk with God is simple but not necessarily easy. You may have a Bible, but you need to actually open it regularly and spend time engaged in its pages. We relate to the eternal God in actual moments in our lives. Every day we have 24 hours. But day after day can quickly fly away without spending repeated time with God.

Listening to God is about hearing the voice of God. Every Christian needs to hear his voice. His presence calms our fears. His Word gives us power to face whatever situations confront us. His encouragement makes all the difference. I can talk to him, but it is he who brings more to the relationship than I do. The psalmist wrote:

> For who is God besides the LORD? And who is the Rock except our God?
>
> It is God who arms me with strength and makes my way perfect.
>
> He makes my feet like the feet of a deer; he enables me to stand on the heights.
>
> He trains my hands for battle; my arms can bend a bow of bronze.
>
> You give me your shield of victory, and your right hand sustains me; you stoop down to make me great.
>
> You broaden the path beneath me, so that my ankles do not turn.
>
> (Psalm 18:31-36)

The voice of God, his Word, is to be central in our lives. The pages of the Bible have been inspired by the Holy Spirit. Our relationship with God brands us to act a certain way and believe certain truths. We get closer to God as we listen to what he is telling us, as the power of the Holy Spirit transforms us. The wind blows. God speaks and changes us.

Listening to God sometimes happens in the familiar dimension. We live life before God. As we walk with him, sometimes a Scripture passage just comes into your mind. Maybe you memorized a Bible passage and suddenly that passage comes to your mind to remind you of God's will for a situation. I remember being in Manhattan on September 11, 2001. I saw the burning buildings. I saw people unglued and scared. I was scared. But all day, Bible passages flooded my mind. The familiar walk was even closer to God as he was speaking his Word into my ears.

But without the discipline of an intentional habit of listening to God, those Scriptures don't have the chance to take root. I remember my Grandma Reyenga. She died at 101. In her last years of life, she was a beautiful demonstration of a saint near the Lord. When you talked with her, she would quote one memorized Scripture verse after another. She lost much of her sight, but she did not need it because she knew God's Word. It was as if her home-discipleship walk had so filled her familiar walk with God that I could not tell the difference between the intentional and the familiar.

A home-discipleship habit of listening to God includes such activities as reading, listening to, or meditating on Scripture passages or Bible-based devotional readings. This may include Bible memorization. This may include listening to a sermon on tape of a Christian radio minister. You may read an encouraging book that is based in Christ.

I would call these intentional acts "listening" to God on a personal level. It is important to have your personal walk well grounded in the Bible. There are several Bible-reading plans that you can adopt as your own. (Appendix C will give you three worthwhile options.) Many times, your intentional listening to God has direct application to your life situation. Many more times, your listening to God is just that. You want to hear what God is saying just because he is talking. His voice is worth listening to. Sometimes it is excellent for us to hear how he had the people of Israel observe dietary laws as found in Leviticus. You may not receive lots of practical application, but you will know more about who God is and his unfolding plan of salvation.

Your personal walk with God does not take place in a vacuum. Your marriage connection, your family connection, your like-minded friend connection, your church connection, and the kingdom connection will all influence how well you listen to God in your familiar walk with him. In return, your personal walk will inform and strengthen your other connections. You cannot neglect a personal walk and attempt to have a family walk or church walk, but neither can you succeed at a personal walk all on your own. We will explore in later chapters how all the connections intertwine.

Home-Discipleship Barriers

Having a repeated talking and listening relationship with God is not as easy as you might think. Modern culture very much challenges the repeated practice of home discipleship. Many Christians are having difficulty practicing home discipleship. A recent Gallup survey put it this way:

> And the percentage of frequent readers, that is, those who read the Bible at least once a week, has decreased slightly over the last decade, from 40% in 1990 to 37% today. 16% of Americans say that they read the Bible every day, 21% say they read it weekly, 12% say they read the Bible monthly, 10% say less than monthly and 41% say that they rarely or never read the Bible. (www.gallup.com)

The fact is that for a nation that has over 400,000 Christian churches, the frequency of Bible reading is hurting. If you asked most Christians if they "feel" good about the infrequency of their home-discipleship walk, most would sense that something was lacking. Today more than ever, we actually have to be intentional about our home discipleship.

How does one make a practical plan of home discipleship that will succeed? Practicing intentional home discipleship starts with an honest evaluation of your personal habits and patterns.

You can feel guilty for not having intentional home discipleship. You can feel helpless for not being able to change. You can blame others for sidetracking your walk with God. You can wish you lived in a different time or different country. But at some point, if you haven't done it yet, you need to take personal responsibility for actually succeeding in doing your home-discipleship walk in your personal life.

The first step to a healthy home-discipleship pattern is to do a self-evaluation. Get a sheet of paper and a pen and answer the following questions:

- Do you have a habitual time of practicing home discipleship in your personal life (structured ways of talking and listening to God daily)? If so, when?
- Do you have someone holding you accountable to practice home discipleship in your personal life? If yes, who?
- Do you have specific habits of memorizing Scripture in your home discipleship? If yes, when do you memorize Scripture?
- When you fail at maintaining home discipleship in your personal life do you:
  —get motivated to start over?
  —get cynical in your struggle?
  —blame others for interrupting your home-discipleship pattern?
- What are typical walls that block you from practicing home discipleship in your personal life?
  —Are you cynical about succeeding because of your past failures?
  —Are you having trouble prioritizing your time?
  —Do you have a barrier in your relationship with God? (A sin barrier? A hurt barrier? A confusion barrier? Other barriers?)

Of what did you become self-aware in doing the question-naire? In order to get healthy in your home discipleship, you need to know those areas of weakness. The reason you investigate this is not to make you feel worse but to know how to develop a plan and to make goals to succeed in your personal connection to God.

Developing a Personal Home-Discipleship Plan

Maybe you have tried to develop a personal home-discipleship plan in the past. Many have tried various discipleship programs. Some have tried programs that encouraged forty days of spiritual walking with God. When the forty days were finished, so was the pattern. In putting together a home-discipleship plan for your personal life, keep a few things in mind. You want your plan to be sustainable and reproducible.

Sustainable Home Discipleship

What makes a habit sustainable? One crucial aspect is to tie a new habit to a habit you are already good at. Brushing your teeth, for instance, is a very sustainable habit. You have a predictable time for doing your brushing. You mostly brush your teeth shortly after you wake up and shortly before you go to bed. What if you were asked to brush your teeth only at 2:00 a.m.? Do you think that you could sustain that habit? Some of us might love good breath and good teeth enough to brush at that time. You would set your alarm clock and get up to brush. But most of us would only get to it occasionally. The point is that brushing your teeth is sustainable largely because it is tied to the habit of waking up and falling to sleep. I have experienced and observed that Christians who are able to sustain their personal home discipleship will practice their home discipleship at habitual times daily—tied to habits such as waking up, arriving at work, lunch break, dinner time, or bed time.

Another aspect of making home discipleship sustainable is choosing a plan that takes into account who you are. Let's say you are not a reader. If you pick a plan with three chapters of Bible reading each day, you will not likely succeed for long. Let's say you have an hour daily commute; you might want to get the Bible on CD or tape. Let's say you are one who has very little personal time. You might want to place a Bible right next to your toilet. You may laugh, but the key is to create a plan that you can actually succeed at! What may start out as "pathetic" can blossom into new and exciting patterns of home discipleship.

A third aspect of making home discipleship sustainable is a supportive environment. Will your spouse join you in being accountable for setting up patterns of personal home discipleship? Maybe you can set up a recognition system for doing your home discipleship, such as a checklist on the refrigerator. We have something similar in our church: Each family has a family banner where family members place a pin when they accomplish certain personal home-discipleship goals. We'll look closer at recognition as a support tool in a later chapter. The point is that a supportive environment is very important to sustain a walk with God in a world that does not care whether you spend any time with God.

A final aspect of making personal home discipleship sustainable is staying within the time allotted in your schedule. Let's say you realistically have fifteen minutes every day for personal discipleship, but you feel guilty about that. So when you do your personal discipleship, you spend one hour. What happens to most people is that they will choose to do home discipleship, then, only when they think they have one full hour. In the process, less home discipleship actually happens.

Here are a few sustainable options for talking and listening to God each day in your personal life:

111

- Set your alarm clock fifteen minutes earlier than you normally get out of bed. Adopt a Bible-reading plan in which you might read or meditate on Scripture for five minutes each day. Then spend five minutes praying. If you do not have memorization happening at any other time in your life, spend five minutes memorizing a Bible passage.
- A great memorization tool is to print out a memory verse and affix it to often-seen places in your house like a kitchen wall, a bathroom wall or next to your bed. You could tape a verse on the ceiling of your bedroom, and when you lie in bed or wake up you would see the verse there.
- Buy a pocket Bible. If you have a lot of waiting to do, read your Bible in line. You could memorize a verse waiting in rush-hour traffic or at the grocery store. You might have a very predictable time that could be harvested for great Bible habits.
- My wife likes to do her personal discipleship at the breakfast table. At our home, people get up at different times, so everyone often eats breakfast alone. (We have our family meal together at night, which we'll talk more about in a later chapter.) If you have breakfasts to yourself, you might be able to feed your soul as well as your body.
- Copy out parts of the Bible. This is a very powerful intentional tool of home discipleship. It allows you to pay attention to every word and not just skim a passage. When you give this kind of depth of attention to God's Word, you will find that certain words and ideas will jump off the pages and strengthen your walk with God.

Reproducible Home Discipleship

As you put together your home-discipleship plan, keep in

mind how reproducible it is. You want to pass on this habit to friends and neighbors, even to your children. You want to encourage others to try what you're doing, to share what you're learning, and to support one another in your goals. If your goal is to spend an hour reading the Bible and an hour praying each day, it will be difficult to create a network of support. When we live in a world where the vast majority of Christians struggle to spend even five minutes a day reading the Bible and praying, the place we must start is mastering fifteen minutes a day in our personal lives. I am not saying that two hours of devotions is bad. But as we get deeper into the connections we will see that spreading our devotional time among marriage, family, and like-minded friends will be much more beneficial than only increasing our time of personal devotions. We need to succeed in a repeatable pattern and then reproduce that pattern with others.

Keeping your devotional pattern simple is important, because talking and listening to God is ultimately simple. Many times we can get caught up in the embellishments and confuse a new believer about what is really taking place. I remember once I was teaching a new Christian about prayer. I thought prayer was a very straightforward exercise. I saw my dad model prayers at the dinner table growing up. I saw others lead prayer. I kind of knew how to take a prayer up, fly around, and then land that prayer with an *Amen*. I do not mean disrespect by characterizing prayer this way. What I found is that this new Christian did not know if she was praying right. At first, I could hardly believe it. I had to tell her that you don't need to use flowery language or preachy verbiage. All you need to do is talk to God in your own words, in your own language. I remember her saying, "How do I know that God hears my prayers?" I told her, "Just pray and see if God shows up." She laughed and began on a prayer walk that has become strong.

Reading the Bible can also be confusing to reproduce. Some

Christians share their devotional pattern and it blows a new Christian out of the water. Be careful to point out that the Bible is the living Word of God, and that just reading it will produce fruit—even if you don't "feel" you get something out of it every time you read a passage. The home-discipleship practice will still benefit you over time. The key message is that God speaks to you through his Word!

Chapter 6

A MAJOR shift has occurred as to how Americans think about marriage. The shift has influenced every area of practice of this institution. From how a boy meets a girl to how someone holds a wedding to how someone lives out the marriage covenant—everything has changed dramatically in the last fifty years. Parts of this chapter will come off as judgmental to many, but I am not picking on you and how you have started your marriage or how you live it now. I want to point out that something has drifted in recent years and that most of Christianity is not aware of this shift.

Take how a boy meets a girl today. It used to be that families knew each other in a faith community. The church socials and family contacts were the primary way a couple would meet each other. Families were deeply involved in the process. After World War II, a dating culture developed in which a young man or woman would "date" several potential young men or women hoping to find true love. Churchgoing folks participated in this shift. By the 1960s, dating started to include sexual expectations. By the turn of the century, saving virginity for marriage had become a minority reality. What used to be called promiscuity is now often heralded as "tension relief," or "trying things out." This is a major shift in one generation.

Many Christians have adopted the nonbeliever method of meeting and getting to know each other. Many Christians meet their potential spouses at bars or nightclubs. Many Christians have given away the ground that sexual contact is exclusive to marriage. Many churchgoers are now living together. Some denominations and churches are trying to redefine marriage to include same-sex couples.

Take a mainstream "Christian" wedding day in North America. They often look just like nonbeliever weddings. There are a few differences; there may still be a Christian pastor with a shortened ceremony. The receptions in particular are drifting away from indigenous Christian culture. The flowing alcohol and the disc jockey are replacing the Christian couple as the center of attention at their wedding celebration.

It used to be that when Christians married, they married in a church. The spiritual flavor of the ceremony also captivated the reception. The main event of the reception was congratulatory; the newly married couple was the center of that event. There may have been a dance, but it was an expression of the family culture. Many receptions took place in the church building and, in lieu of a dance, the guests might put on a program that celebrates the life of the couple. At the program, Scripture was read or recited. There was singing. There might be skits. The wedding day reflected the Christian cultural heritage that would be a great witness and testimony of what godly marriage was all about.

Today there seem to be American-culture wedding packages. The wedding packages are costly. Popular movies like *Father of the Bride* are like advertising for what is expected. The internet is ablaze with products and services selling the perfect wedding day. One such website, Mike's Art Wedding, reported the amount of money you can expect to pay:

> Weddings cost 18% more than just four years ago. *Wilton Wedding 2003 marketing reporting, Brides Magazine,* and *Wedding Magazine* estimate the national (USA) average cost for a wedding at $20,000 to $25,000. Our calculator is based on an average number of guests, and varies by region. We do not include the honeymoon. Our calculator will calculate your budget based on the national with regional effects. (2005)

Twenty to twenty-five thousand dollars is enough to pay off those student loans or to put a down payment on a house. I am not saying that Christians should never spend money on weddings, but I am saying that we should not spend money just because our "branded" culture tells us we should.

The cultural drift has affected our attitudes toward the purposes of marriage. In the past, most wedding ceremonies included verses concerning propagating the earth. The idea that having children is one of God's primary purposes for marriage is highly disfavored today. Many Christians are having fewer and fewer children. Most Christians assume that birth control is a "no brainer" in marriage. Two children and one dog or a cat is what many Christians believe is the allotment that God desires for their household. This is a huge shift from the historical belief that contraception was not to be used or only in special circumstances.

Notions about divorce have changed. In the early part of the last century, divorce was rare. People could go a whole year without even meeting a divorced person. Today, no-fault divorce is commonplace even among Christians.

What is happening? Marriages are drifting away from God's instructions for marriage. Christians are detaching their marriages from the biblical institution of what marriage is intended to be. The price is high. Christian marriages are breaking up, and children are subjected to the pain of these separations. What can be done?

I believe that Christians need to acknowledge God as Lord of their marriage union. This will happen when a Christian couple understands that God relates spiritually to the marriage couple. If you are married, you walk together before God in that union. The Word of God has transforming power in your marriage walk. Home discipleship at the marriage-walk level keeps your marriage bathed in God's Word and prayer. Home discipleship greatly inspires your day-to-day marriage lifestyle.

When couples marry "in the Lord," they marry into a committed relationship with God as the center of their marriage. This means that the voice of God guides the marriage. This also means that as a married couple, the husband and wife respond in prayer to God.

Just as with the personal connection, the marriage connection has a familiar walk and a home-discipleship walk. The familiar walk before God very much connects to the familiar walk between man and woman. This includes the everyday talking and listening between husband and wife—"Hi honey, I'm home," "Hubby, will you take the dog for a walk?" "Dear, I love you!"—in which each spouse surrenders daily in love for each other. The familiar marriage walk not only walks in the kitchen and living room; a couple can take a stroll into the bedroom and without even being that intentional about it, engage in marital relations. This marriage walk even happens when a couple may be away from each other; the wedding ring says that this man and this woman are walking with a specific person.

In life, a marriage walk can drift, too. The familiar walk needs the support of an intentional walk—a specific commitment of time for going deeper into talking and listening repeatedly. Husband and wife strengthen their marriage through a planned night out or a planned romantic evening. Sometimes these intentional times of talking and listening are problem-solving in nature. Sometimes these talks recount the couple's history: "Remember when we first met?" Intentional focus on each other and open personal revelation are common elements in taking time out to build the marriage.

What does this have to do with a spiritual marriage walk? The Word of God shapes both the familiar and intentional marriage walks. When husband and wife open the Bible on a regular basis, God's Word and Spirit impact the man and the woman—the marriage.

The familiar and intentional marriage walks are blessed by God through his Word as his Spirit continues to soften the spouses' hearts for each other. This happens when individuals are walking with God. This also happens when a couple opens up the Bible and prays together. God's Word speaks to every area of the marriage walk. God's presence draws the couple into a closer partnership and union. And when God is the center of a marriage, the marriage grows in love and power. This communion with God and his Word keeps a marriage from drifting away from the object of worship: namely, Christ.

What benefits does a strong spiritual marriage walk bring to a Christian couple? Your marriage no longer serves merely your own interests. The marriage walk is done in a relationship with God. God will lead a married couple into great purpose and happiness. His presence will change any marriage if the married couple will yield to him.

The Home-Discipleship Marriage Walk

What is home discipleship in a marriage? It is simply a husband and wife intentionally talking to God together and listening together to God's Word for their marriage. It is the repeated practice of praying aloud together before God and reading the Bible together.

A century ago, it was commonplace for Christian couples to pray and read God's Word together. When Christian couples married, they were encouraged to intentionally practice home discipleship at the marriage level. In a book written in the late nineteenth century, J.R. Miller encouraged married couples in intentional home discipleship. He wrote:

> They [the married couple] should read [the Bible and other Christian books] and study together, having the same line of thought, helping each other toward a higher mental culture. They should worship together, praying side by side, communing on the holiest themes of life and hope, and together carrying to God's feet the burdens of their hearts for their children and for every precious object. Why should they not talk together of their personal trials, their peculiar temptations, their infirmities, and help each other by sympathy, by brave word and by intercession, to be victorious in living? (*Home-Making*, 1882)

Some of you may have heard of stories of Christian grandparents or even great-grandparents who would read passages from Scripture before going to bed and then kneel at the bedside together. There is something very powerful about ending your day in God's Word and in prayer together.

Does God bless you as you intentionally talk to him and listen to him as a married couple? Over the years, those who practiced home discipleship in this way reported some very practical benefits to their marriage:

- "God often has spoken to us together about a decision we need to make."
- "We find that we need to talk out any conflict we are struggling with because we are not going to go before the Lord in conflict. This has really helped our marriage."

- "We will spend a few minutes reading a devotional, then a few minutes reading a book on marriage. Then we pray together. Within fifteen minutes we get a daily marriage boost, but more than that, we feel our marriage is being filled with God's presence."
- "We find that our marital relations have even increased significantly, and more children are born." (This one is quite commonly reported.)
- "We find that we have a forum now to include God in our parenting discussions. We talk about our children and their needs. We read the Bible. We pray. We get answers!"
- "God comforted us in our loss."
- "Our marriage flame was rekindled."
- "Some worldly understandings were gradually dealt with. These understandings were hurting our marriage."
- "My husband has started to act more kind and romantic toward me since we started praying and reading the Bible together. He thinks of my emotional needs so differently. I have a renewed love for that man."
- "My wife takes more interest in my sexual needs now. I thought that sexuality in marriage was somehow dirty. I did not think that this was an area that God specifically was interested in. I was so wrong. My wife is a Solomon bride now. Wow."
- "My husband became a believer through the Word of God. He found out that God is actually there when you talk and listen to him together."

Why does this happen? When you practice home discipleship as a married couple, you specifically invite God into your marriage connection. There is not one centimeter that God's reign and blessing do not extend over. His Word does not return void. His presence will do for you what great amounts of human counseling will not accomplish: God will break down walls that you cannot in your own strength. God will stop your marriage from drifting. God will help you in ways you will experience only as you practice home discipleship. This practice will transform your familiar walk with each other and your familiar walk with God.

Overcoming the Obstacles

My wife and I started practicing marriage home discipleship together more than fifteen years ago. At first it was hard to sustain. We often could not find a time when both of us could meet. Often we went to bed at different times. When we did do our devotions, sometimes they would take so long that it affected the next time. We would resist doing them every night because we were secretly concerned about how long they were going to take and cut into our sleep. In the early days, one or both of us would not feel like reading the Bible together for whatever reason. We started and stopped. We felt great about getting together, but we also failed enough to get us frustrated.

After about two years of prayerfully struggling over what to do, we finally figured out some important principles for succeeding at practicing home discipleship at the marriage level.

Pick a Time and Stick to it

My wife and I discovered that we needed to go to bed at the same time. This is a time that works for both of us. My wife was originally a morning person. I would like to stay up late. We needed to find a time that both of us could live with. The simple decision to go to bed at the same time had important benefits. Now we could tie the habit of marriage devotions to bedtime. We simply read a series of verses from the Bible. Sometimes we will read a few pages from an excellent resource book. Then I will pray first. I end my prayer with "In Jesus' name." Pam can either keep praying or just say, "Amen."

Maybe the bedtime pattern is just not going to work for you. Each couple is different. You might not always know what pattern is going to stick for you. You may find that you will try up to five different scenarios before you find the one that works for you. Many who attempt home discipleship at the marriage level give up too easily in finding a time that will actually work for them.

Over the years, several great time options have been suggested by couples who have succeeded in marriage home discipleship. Here are some for you to consider:

- Wake up fifteen minutes earlier every morning.
- Meet for 10:00 p.m. ice cream and discipleship.
- Some people take a while to wake up. Get a CD of the whole Bible or a godly marriage resource on tape and keep it in your room. Once the alarm goes off, start listening to Scripture together, and before you get out of bed, pray.
- Tie aspects of home discipleship to marital relations. Conclude a time of marital intimacy with each other with prayer.
- Some couples practice home discipleship over the phone.

Your situation will be your situation. If you search hard enough, you will discover a time. At first it will be challenging to start the new habit, but stick with it. Stay focused.

Committing to Following Through

When you are first getting into this new pattern, you will find you need to put into your marriage some special measures. The fact is that one or both of you will try to sabotage your new marriage home-discipleship practice. The man is called by God to be the head of his wife, so, men, you are responsible. I remember when I realized that I was responsible to God to lead my marriage and home into home-discipleship practices. I was over-whelmed at first. What if I fail? After failing a few times, I began to realize that failure was not an option. My wife, Pam, and I met to discuss how we were going to succeed at practicing home discipleship in our marriage no matter what. This was an interest-ing meeting. I admitted that I needed God's help and her help in making sure that we actually succeeded. That's when we had to make some decisions like going to bed at the same time. We both admitted we might feel tired and either one of us would be capa-ble of flaking out at those times. In fact, we admitted to many times when we were capable of not supporting the practice of home discipleship. We made a covenant with each other:

- We would go to bed at the same time. If Pam wanted to go to bed early, I would tuck her in after we practiced home discipleship.

- If either of us did not "feel" like practicing home disciple-ship, the other would be deputized to take charge to make sure that home discipleship happened. The person deputized would not make the other feel demeaned or guilty. Unemotional leadership here is very important. Do not duplicate this dialogue: "I see you're going to bed early; I'm going to stay up and watch the news." The other spouse: "What? I thought we were going to do home discipleship. How many times are you going to drop the ball? You say you love God but you don't show it." Instead you might respond more like this: "OK, but we need to do devotions before I go to sleep." No matter what excuse one of us gives, the other will not buy it, nor make the person feel bad for trying to use the excuse.

- We would not go to bed angry at each other. You can't pray to God angry at each other.

- We would keep each other's spiritual, emotional, and

124

sexual needs as a loving, prayerful, and active priority.

At first these commitments were difficult to keep. There was much in our own sinful nature that warred against this commitment to each other. There was much spiritual warfare, too. At first, it felt like "law." It was almost artificial. But once we established the habit, it wasn't long before home discipleship felt normal and natural. We didn't have to struggle but were able to just enjoy it. We eventually came to look forward to it.

Sustainability

Fifteen minutes of intentional home discipleship is very sustainable. This is in addition to the fifteen minutes of personal devotional time, but much of what you do together can overlap. Perhaps if you read the same Bible passage on your own, you can share your favorite verse or idea in the passage and read those to each other. If you have a prayer that God answered that day, you can share how God worked in your day. If you memorized a verse on your own, recite it together. The idea is not to create a separate task but to strengthen and support your personal habit with your marriage habit.

At the same time, you don't want your spiritual marriage walk simply to rehash your personal devotions; add in a habit or practice that is specific to your marriage, such as reading from a marriage devotional or a section from a Christian marriage book. Hold hands. Celebrate your union before God. Pray aloud together.

Fifteen minutes a day is a sustainable and reproducible habit. In fifteen minutes, you and your spouse can connect with God and each other where real discipleship occurs. If that sounds like too much, start with five or ten minutes and see what happens. If fifteen minutes doesn't seem like much, try starting with only fifteen minutes and make sure you can sustain that, so you do not end up skipping marriage discipleship for fear it will rob you of sleep. Fifteen minutes a day multiplied by one year means you are spending more than 91 hours together—more than two work weeks just worshipping God as a couple. That will make a big impact on your familiar spiritual walks both individually and as a married couple!

The Husband's Responsibility

The Bible places the man as the spiritual head of his home. Discussion continues to rage about what this means. Some Christians understand "headship" as male domination or control. Others have thrown headship completely out the door, and placed as much (if not more) responsibility for the spiritual health of the family on the woman. In many churches, you see mainly women and children attending. Where are the men?

The teaching of biblical male headship has fallen on difficult times. Most news outlets have treated this teaching as caveman thinking when it has become an issue in the national spotlight. Even many in the Christian church have questioned this teaching. Some have questioned it openly, even doubting that the Bible really says that the husband is the head of his wife. Most have questioned this teaching by their actions. Many Christian men who are called to be the head of their home agree with what the Bible says but in reality do not take their responsibility seriously. The Bible does teach about headship, and God expects the husband to take responsibility for leading his wife and family. Ephesians 5:22b says:

> For the husband is the head of the wife as Christ is the head of
> the church, his body, of which he is the Savior.

Men, this truth ought to humble you to your knees. Your wife and children are put into your care. You are responsible. What does it mean that you are the head? Jesus once defined importance and headship to his disciples. They were arguing about who was the greatest. They were concerned about who was going to be in charge.

> Sitting down, Jesus called the Twelve and said, "If anyone wants to be first, he must be the very last, and the servant of all." (Mark 9:35)

Here are a few questions for Christian husbands: Are you leading your wife into the kingdom of God? Or are you leading her into frustration and ruin? Have you turned off the sports game and turned on the real contest—a marriage that is walking with God? So many wives have difficulty with the headship principle because their husband's leadership is not godly. Wives are called to submit to you as is "fitting in the Lord" (Colossians 3:18). But sometimes your leadership is weak and worldly. Some may argue, "I'm making a living. I'm feeding the family. I am not having an affair." Great! But are you leading your wife in home discipleship? Are you listening to her? A great leader does not micromanage. A great leader helps those in his charge to maximize the gifts God has given them. A great leader sees the gifts of his wife and gives her the responsibility and authority to get things done as his kingdom partner. A great husband does not use "headship" to get his way. A great husband is the responsible head to lead in God's way. But he himself must lead as one connected to God.

A husband must understand that the word *submit* applies to him. He must submit to God. "Submit yourselves, then, to God," says James 4:7a. God will hold you accountable for how you lead your wife. Will you bring her down to ruin? Will you bring her to heights she never dreamed of? Marriage is an institution made by God. As a husband, you are called to lead in the Lord! I am glad "in the Lord" is key in understanding headship. Headship leadership is based in love. Scripture makes that clear:

> Husbands, love your wives, just as Christ loved the church and gave himself up for her. (Ephesians 5:25)

God is watching your leadership. Self-centered leadership is not biblical headship. Self-centered leadership brings only exasperation. Husbands, when you lead in home discipleship, lead your wife to the feet of Jesus. She will follow!

Wives and Submission

Wives, do you like the word "submit"? Maybe you do or maybe you do not. It can seem like foolishness for one person to submit to another person just because he is male. That is not why you submit. You submit because God wants you to. The submission passages are clear:

> Wives, submit to your husbands, as is fitting in the Lord. (Colossians 3:18)

> Wives, submit to your husbands as to the Lord. (Ephesians 5:22)

The word "submit" does not mean that you do whatever your husband wants you to do. It means that you respect him and seek to follow his lead. What about times he asked you to sin? If you are led into sin, you sin against one who is a higher authority than your husband. Therefore, you will not submit to that. And when you do resist submitting to your husband in these cases, keep a submissive attitude, like Daniel, who did not submit to the authority of the king in the book of Daniel but did so with respect.

When it comes to home discipleship, submitting to your husband means that you follow him as he leads you into the kingdom of heaven. If he wants to lead you and the family in devotions, you will gladly follow. If he will not lead you in home discipleship, you will still need to practice home discipleship in your personal life and with the children. But you are still called to live in submission to him as the head of your marriage and home.

I have seen unbelieving men come to the Lord because of the submissive example of their wives. That Bible passage 1 Peter 3:1 is right on:

> Wives, in the same way be submissive to your husbands so that, if any of them do not believe the Word, they may be won over without words by the behavior of their wives.

I remember one time a new Christian wife shared with me that for a long time her husband wanted just sex and food. But her story had a happy ending. She recounted it something like this:

> I have to admit that one reason I met the Lord is out of feeling used in giving my husband sex and food. After becoming a Christian, something happened to me. My own heart was broken down to be submissive to God. I heard the command to be submissive to my husband and that give me some trouble at first. I read every passage about submission and came upon the one in 1 Peter 3:1. I set my heart to win my husband over by my behavior. My husband was very wary of my new commitment to Christ. He was worried that I was going to turn into a prude from reading the Bible. Instead, I prayed to the Lord to make me submissive to him as was fitting in the Lord.
>
> Some things happened to me. I started to really love him. I knew that he liked sex and food, and I gave it to him in a voluntary way like never before. He did not know what happened to me. He actually started to encourage me to read the Bible more and attend church. The more I became submissive to him, the more he started asking questions about his own life. Soon he would ask questions about what I was reading in the Bible. He permitted me to read the Bible at the table with the kids. He was listening. I closed our meals with prayer. I asked him if he would

read the Bible while I nursed one of our babies. He agreed. Soon he was reading the Bible. As he became closer to God, I was even more submissive to him. I was a woman at peace with God and my husband.

My husband was struggling. He had no peace and wanted what I had. The more my life was being transformed by God, the more he became jealous of my joy. My husband started to attend church with us. He read more and more of the Bible. He became a Christian man, husband, and father. Every time we read the Bible together or pray together, my heart skips a beat! I have seen the power of submission. I saw that power first displayed in Christ's submission to the will of the Father to die on the cross for me. I could lay down my life for my husband in my service for Christ. God blessed it. And I have a Christian man to follow now.

There is power is submission. What you and your husband are called to do is be a mighty team to promote the kingdom of God. Your husband is responsible to lead, and you are responsible to submit in the Lord.

Let's get very practical now about issues in getting a home-discipleship walk going in your marriage and how that relates to headship and submission. Many wives have been used to leading the home spiritually. The reason you did it was because your husband was not leading you or the family in this area. Now your husband is starting to step up and lead. But you have seen him start and stop things in the past. You wonder whether this marriage home-discipleship thing is just another one of his fads. In fact, you are cautious now in how you follow your husband. Much is at stake in your following your husband. Here are some suggestions that will really help him succeed at being the spiritual leader of your home:

- Commit to follow his lead in setting up home discipleship in your home.

- When he forgets to lead you in this on a specific day, gently bring up the subject in a respectful way: "Dear, I know that you want us to do our devotions. Shall I get the Bible out?"
- Pray for your husband rather than criticize him.

Getting your Plan Together

Now it is time to get your marriage home-discipleship plan in place. Together answer the following questions and come up with a plan for your marriage spiritual walk:

- At what time are you going to practice home discipleship each day?
- What discipleship material are you going to use?
- What obstacles do you see that will hurt your plans?
- How are you going to put a plan in place that takes those obstacles into account?
- Who is someone you can share your marriage plan with, who will keep you accountable?
- Do you need a reward system? What rewards will you choose to recognize your new home-discipleship habits?

Chapter 7

Connection Three:
The Family Connection

IMAGINE THE world four hundred years from now, assuming Christ has not yet returned. You are long gone from the earth. But something you started or passed on is still happening. You passed on a walk with God to your children. You have been very careful to pass on a familiar walk and an intentional home-discipleship walk. You also made sure that they could reproduce their walk in the very secular world that will confront the generations that come after you. Your children have seen the generational vision. Your children have passed it on to their children. They have passed it on to their children. This walk has been passed on now for twenty generations. You have millions of descendants now. And here is the good news: There are now millions of home-discipled witnesses of Christ awaiting Christ's coming.

By starting home discipleship in your family and making it reproducible, you are starting intentional practices that will place the Bible and prayer in a central role for millions of descendants not yet born. If you have two children, and each of your children have two children, and so forth, in twenty generations that will add up to over one million descendants. Many of you have more than two children; imagine your descendants.

> So the next generation would know them, even the children yet
> to be born, and they in turn would tell their children. Then they
> would put their trust in God. (Psalm 78:6-7a)

This powerful dream for the future is grounded in the reality you practice today. It matters how you lead your family in home discipleship. It matters how you help each of your children thrive in a reproducible walk. It matters that what you do when your children are young will stay with them and that they will pass these practices on to the next generation.

You must be self-aware of the question of what you pass on to the next generation. If you are unfocused about what you seek to pass on to the next generation, you may find that what passes on is not what you'd hoped. In home discipleship, you will find that some of what you pass on will be "caught" (your children observing how you live) and some things will be "taught" (specific instructions your children will follow). Both the "caught" and the "taught" come as a family walks with God. Remember what a walk with God is: A walk with God has a familiar side and an intentional discipleship side.

The Shifting Priorities of the Familiar Walk

Every family has a familiar family walk. The familiar walk in the family is demonstrated in how each person treats the others. It is demonstrated in how the family actually gets along. The familiar walk of a family includes those family habits that occur every day: eating meals together, play time, time in the car doing errands, praying together before bedtime. The familiar family walk in many ways is the culture of your family, your interaction with each other and God. Many lessons of godliness and life are being taught and caught as Christian family members interact with each other and with God.

But many Christian families have drifted in their spiritual walks. The way the family gets along with each other is not that different from how unbelieving families get along. I know of Christian families where the fathers are not interested in spending time with their children. They are more interested in sports or work than in creating space to relate to their children. Some studies suggest that the average father spends only eight to ten minutes a day with his children—and this includes television and meal times. (Victor Lee and Jerry Pipes quote statistics from American Family Association research to this effect in their 1999 book *Family to Family*.) Others studies paint an even darker picture. Patrick Morley's 1992 book *The Man in the Mirror* suggests that the average American father spends thirty-seven seconds a day with his children. How can we calculate the negative impact this is having in our families?

Many mothers are now working. The last sixty years have seen a major shift in the amount of time mothers spend with the family. Dr. Lois Wladis Hoffman notes these statistics:

Labor force participation rates of mothers with children under 18, 1940 and 1946-1996:
- 1940, 8.6%
- 1946, 18.2%
- 1956, 27.5%
- 1966, 35.8%
- 1976, 48.8%
- 1986, 62.5%
- 1996, 70.0%

(The Effects of the Mother's Employment on the Family and the Child, 1998)

This has had a major effect on the familiar walk of modern families. Families are often very fragmented. With Mom gone many hours of the week, the family notices the impact on the family walk. Many mothers feel great amounts of stress in trying to balance their time between the family and work. It is no wonder that birth rates have plummeted. Mothers are becoming too busy to bear children. Children have become inconvenient.

The drift has also occurred in family size. The Bible is very clear about being fruitful and multiplying. More and more the standard family size has become two children. After years of hearing about overpopulation concerns and a lack of resources to support a growing world, the media has recently been talking about the threats of depopulation and its effect on society. Scott Burns wrote an article called "Why we're not having enough babies" published on MSN Money in 2004, in which he wrote:

> "We're not facing a nuclear war or a population bomb; we're facing a depopulation bomb. This isn't just Europe. It's the entire world."
>
> That was one of the first things Phillip Longman said when I called to talk about his book, "The Empty Cradle: How Falling Birthrates Threaten World Prosperity (And What to Do About It)." I called him because he is one of the few economic writers whose vision includes families as something more than consuming units. He clearly recognizes that families are powerful economic institutions in their own right. Without families—and all they do to create and prepare the next generation—our market economy and public-service economy would collapse.

Burns notes that the birth rate of 3.7 births per woman in 1957 in America has fallen to just over the 2.1 births needed to maintain a level population. In Europe, the birth rates are even lower, meaning that by 2050 the population will dwindle back to its 1950 levels.

The drift in family culture has extended even to the definition of the word "family." The traditional definition used to be a

136

father and mother with children. Because of skyrocketing divorce rates and sexual promiscuity, we have a proliferation of single-parent families, families who split time between two homes, and other blended families.

Canada has been approving legislation that redefines marriage and the family. The new definition completely destroys the traditional understanding of family. Brian Watts wrote an article for the Christian website U-Turn.net titled, "Is There a Future for the Family?" He reflected on Canada's redefinition of the family this way:

> But the legislation had the *effect* of reducing the definition of marriage to two (or more) people living together in any arrangement, with or without children, for whatever reason.

For many, the family is just whatever they want it to be. They can call it a family if they hang out together for whatever reason.

Many changes have assaulted the makeup of the family in one generation. These changes have brought many heartaches into the lives of children and parents, husbands and wives. But even more devastating has been the shift in priorities and habits of Christian families. How the Christian family spends its time has changed dramatically. A major priority shift can be noticed even if we go back less than one hundred years.

My dad was born in 1920. His family practiced home discipleship. They ate meals together growing up. After dinner, his father got the Bible out. They memorized passages, and they sang hymns and psalms at home. The family prioritized time together each day like this. If my father's family went to visit a cousin or another member of the church, that family most likely had the same pattern happening at home. I asked my dad why they were so successful at practicing home discipleship back then in comparison with practicing home discipleship today. My dad paused and said, "It was easy. We didn't have anything else to do."

In 1935 rural Wisconsin, three years before electricity, my father's family worked hard. When Grandma spent all day making the food, this was an event that everyone was going to participate in. There was no TV. They did have a radio, but they were limited in how much the radio could run on batteries. After dinner was complete, they opened the Word of God and had a lively discussion to discover what God was saying. Many of the children played instruments. Every number in the hymnbook was learned and many of them in four parts.

My dad's family had a very spiritual familiar walk. In fact, in many ways they would have had a difficult time distinguishing their familiar walk from their intentional or home-discipleship walk. Reading the Bible, praying, memorizing Scripture, singing, and learning to play an instrument were just things that you did. In those days, personal and marriage devotions were often caught up in the family walk. The family was a very powerful unit of home discipleship. The family's priority was family worship, and that environment was a powerful discipleship place for every member of the family.

Many things happened around the time of World War II in my father's family. These things happened in incremental fashion. The radio's role increased in the home after the farm got electricity. The vacant jobs left by departing soldiers brought many women into the work force. After World War II, the post-war prosperity brought new products into most American homes. Soon every home had a TV, and many families gathered around it after their family meal. But even the family meal would be challenged. "TV dinners" could be put in the oven, and you could eat them while you watched television. Soon the microwave made the preparation of food even faster. The family meal would eventually struggle as a daily institution in modern American life.

By 1980, most families were struggling just to sustain time together. The Christian family was struggling, too. I remember my parents insisting that family discipleship occur in our home. At that time, schools and recreational sports still respected the idea of a dinner hour each night. After our meal, the habits of home-discipleship practices occurred on a daily basis. It was still possible to practice home discipleship without taking drastic steps, especially for parents who had been mentored by their parents in home discipleship.

More than twenty-five years later, a family must be counter-cultural in every way to prioritize home discipleship. The accepted values of a typical American family leave no room for connection or walking together. It is easy for Christian families to slip into the desires of wanting their children to be "happy" with their friends or helping them "get ahead" with loads of activities. We have lost the idea that a strong family life is a source of lasting happiness and will serve our children well as they pursue their future. Too often we sacrifice togetherness for the sake of individual interests.

Families eating together at least one meal: Only 34 percent of American families eat one meal together each day. (Victor Lee and Jerry Pipes in *Family to Family*)

Only 12 percent of America's families pray together. (Victor Lee and Jerry Pipes in *Family to Family*)

According to Fr. John Pungente of the Jesuit Communication Project in Toronto, by the time the average North American child graduates from high school, he or she will have:
—watched 15,000 hours of television
—seen 350,000 commercials
—listened to 10,500 hours of pop music
—attended 400 movies

The fact is the typical family has very little time for getting together—and the pace of new technologies to challenge family togetherness is accelerating. Take the use of the internet. The use of the internet is growing much more quickly than all other preceding technologies. The radio was around for thirty-eight years before it boasted 50 million listeners; TV did better and took thirteen years to reach 50 million viewers. The internet passed the 50-million-users mark in only four years (U.S. Commerce Department statistics, cited in the *Ottawa Citizen*, April 16, 1998).

OK, enough facts. You can see that the familiar walk of the typical family is not a walk that promotes discipleship. It does not even promote sustaining anything that looks like a nuclear family. Children are born into homes that are actually hostile to their growing up into the Lord Jesus. The typical home practices a familiar walk that will lead right into the way of death.

What are you going to do about it? How about going back to 1935? This will not work for most of us. Most of us are not going to get rid of our televisions. Most of us will keep the internet. Most of us will continue to have radios. But beware of what these technologies can do to your families. Keeping your TV could be the spiritual death of your children. Keeping the internet could be the spiritual death of your children. You might be taking them to church, but their real values are being shaped by the 15,000 hours of TV that they are watching.

Since it is not 1935, we need to intentionally deploy a home-discipleship walk that will transform our familiar family walk. This home-discipleship walk will need to actually be reproducible and sustainable. We want our children to be able to do it, and we want this walk to be around no matter what technological advances creep into our homes.

*   *   *

The Home-Discipleship Walk in Your Family

The goal of a home-discipleship walk is to place intentional patterns in your family that support each family member's growing relationship to Christ. This will include creating a distinct family culture that prioritizes talking and listening repeatedly to God as a central pattern. When you put this culture in place at first, it will feel strange and different, mainly because your family has become used to a certain familiar family walk. Any time you make a change, it will take a while before it becomes familiar.

Let me remind you of the key elements of home discipleship as it applies to the family: prayer, Bible reading, family memorization, family singing. These elements are repeated on a regular basis to support a Christ-centered growing relationship. Intentional home discipleship creates spiritual proximity for the family to get together and support the spiritual walks of each of the family members. When a family member has an individual struggle, family home discipleship usually illustrates the struggle. For instance, if one of the children does not want to pray at the family level, it usually shows the parents that something needs attention on the personal level.

These elements of family worship have been taught for generations, ever since the Reformation. The *Directory for Family Worship* in early American Presbyterian churches around 1750 did not include Scripture memorization, but it did include prayer, Bible reading, and singing:

> Family worship, which ought to be performed by every family, ordinarily morning and evening, consists in prayer, reading the Scriptures, and singing praises.

The fact is that home discipleship at the family level has been practiced for generations, and our generation also must pursue these elements for our families.

Prayer: Talking to God

When your family prays, you are both walking an intentional home-discipleship walk but you are walking with God in a familiar way as well. When your family memorizes the Lord's Prayer together, it is an intentional effort, but before long it will soon become part of an individual and family familiar walk. The memorizing may feel somewhat artificial at first, but soon that prayer will just be part of who you are and your communication with God. Being intentional demonstrates to your children the priority of talking to God. The family also learns how to pray when prayers are verbally spoken. Family members learn the posture of prayer. All this will soon become part of your familiar walking.

Talking to God through home discipleship is very important for raising children in the Lord. When children come into the world, they are too young to make a decision for Christ. Yet Scripture sees the children as somehow part of the family of God. God has ordained praise out of the mouths of infants (Psalm 8:2). Jesus encouraged the children to come to him and said not to hinder them (Mark 10:13-16). Prayer at the family level is very important to help your children come to God at a young age.

When should you pray as a family? At the family connection level, prayers at habitual times are very effective, along with spontaneous prayers.

- Pray before and after meals, even in restaurants.
- Pray before bedtime. If you have young children, teach them to memorize a prayer that they can say every night. Here's one I learned growing up and that I taught my children when they were young: "Now I lay me down to sleep, I pray to you, Lord, my soul to keep. Angels watch me through the night and bring me safe to morning light. Amen."

- Pray at family holiday celebrations or other occasions, like birthdays or graduations.
- Give special prayers in time of need. Get the whole family together for immediate prayer when there is a crisis that needs it.
- Pray in praise and celebration for any wonderful news or an achievement of a family member.

Essentially, what you are doing is creating a family culture that comes near to God. You are saying that your family is dependent on God. At the family prayer level, you will be able to use the ACTS guide very well. Praying in adoration, confession, thanksgiving, and supplication is a pattern your family can use at any habitual or spontaneous time of prayer.

Praying as a family teaches your children to have a confident prayer life. As you model habitual prayer and participate in spontaneous prayer, your children learn much about talking to God. By the time your children leave the home, they may not be able to distinguish between the home-discipleship intentional activity and the familiar walk with God. This is beautiful.

Bible Reading: Listening to God

God relates to you as a family. The Bible places extreme importance on family history and heritage. He speaks to families as a whole and to each member of the family. When you read the Bible, your family has the opportunity to listen to God. Sometimes God's voice will be immediately practical, giving direction or spurring spiritual transformation. Sometimes you read something in the Bible that helps members of the family learn more about God. The key is that God's Word speaks to your family and its members. God's voice is a welcome sound in a home-discipleship family.

Often families will use a Bible-reading plan. The *Christian*

Leaders Family Journal offers three Bible-reading plans. The option for reading the New Testament in one year or the option of reading 365 key chapters of the Bible in one year are very manageable for family devotions. (Refer to Appendix C to learn more about these options.) We have done both in our family and highly recommend them. This also gives each family member a working understanding of the Bible's message.

Some families will use a family devotional guide. Depending on the leadership of the parents, these guides can be excellent tools for opening up God's Word. My family has used devotional writings as well. The advantage of using devotional writings is that they usually expound immediately on the passage that has been read. This can be very helpful.

The key issue is to open the Word of God. The Bible says that God's Word does not return void but accomplishes its purpose (Isaiah 55:10-11). And God's Word is powerful enough to keep your family's familiar walk from drifting toward idols.

I like what James W. Alexander wrote about the role of the Word of God in home discipleship. He wrote this in his book *Family Worship* in 1847:

> The daily regular and solemn reading of God's holy word, by a parent before his children, is one of the most powerful agencies of a Christian life. We are prone to undervalue this cause. It is a constant dripping, but it wears its mark into the rock. A family thus trained cannot be ignorant of the Word. The whole Scriptures come repeatedly before the mind. The most heedless child must observe and retain some portions of the sacred oracles: the most forgetful must treasure up some passages for life. No one part of juvenile education is more important. Between families thus instructed, and those where the Bible is not read, the contrast is striking. To deny such a source of influence to the youthful mind is an injustice.

Scripture Memory: Listening to God

Scripture memory is a difficult piece to actually accomplish in home discipleship. When we first started memorizing Scripture in our family, it was as if my brain was out of shape. But Scripture memory has been worth the time and effort. The whole family has experienced how God's Word affects our familiar walks time and time again when previously memorized Scripture comes to mind to direct or comfort us in living our lives before the face of God. The Psalmist understood that dynamic of memorizing God's Word:

> I seek you with all my heart; do not let me stray from your commands. I have hidden your word in my heart that I might not sin against you. (Psalm 119:10-11)

The family may be the best place for Scripture memory. You can memorize one Scripture passage each day; it takes less than five minutes. In our church, we have a set time once a month where families recite the passages they've memorized. What I've discovered is that there are many ways for families to memorize one passage a day. Here is the Reyenga system: Someone in the family will say the verse we are memorizing three times while everyone else is listening. Then the whole family will repeat it back three times. Then each person in the family says the verse. We find that everyone is already a long way toward memorizing the verse. The next day we review the previous verse then learn the next one in a chapter. By the end of the month, we know a chapter or section of a chapter. My family already knows hundreds of verses and many, many chapters. Time and time again, those Bible passages we have memorized have helped the individual familiar walk with God in every member of the family.

I recommend that you start memorizing Scripture with the timeless favorites. Turn to Appendix D for more than one hundred suggestions that have worked for many other families.

Family Singing: Talking to God

Many families are singing less at home and becoming spectators in the area of music. This is true on the individual level, the couple level, and the family level. When I grew up in the 1960s and 1970s, I remember families getting together for the singing of hymns. I loved going to these events: We sang hymns that every family was singing at home and at church. The young knew the hymns; the old knew the hymns. Now, it seems that few people know the words to even their most favorite hymns or praise songs. Kids, teenagers, and adults are all learning different songs in their separate ministries within the church. A home-discipleship practice of learning and singing songs together will affect not only the members of your family but the way they worship at church. If the home sings, the church will be vibrant with worship and praise.

I have seen this dynamic throughout my Christian life. I understand more and more what the apostle Paul was getting at in Ephesians 5:19-20:

> Speak to one another with psalms, hymns and spiritual songs. Sing and make music in your heart to the Lord, always giving thanks to God the Father for everything, in the name of our Lord Jesus Christ.

The singing of psalms, hymns, and spiritual songs in your family is a vital part of your home-discipleship practice. Notice how learning new songs fits into the familiar walk and the intentional discipleship walk. When you learn a new song or hymn, it often comes off as a chore. It feels a little artificial. But as you learn it, soon it develops levels of meaning that take the song into the area of your familiar walk. This familiar impact can happen at any setting where you are singing. It might be at work, and a tune to a hymn or praise song is in your mind. All day a song is ministering to you in your personal familiar walk. The same happens in Christian marriage; anytime Pam and I hear or sing the song "My Jesus, I Have Promised to Serve You Till the End," it encourages us in our marriage. This was the marriage hymn we picked at our wedding.

At the family setting, the interplay between the familiar walk and the intentional walk is powerful. I recall my father teaching my then 10-year-old daughter, Christina, the old hymn "In the Sweet Bye and Bye." My father brought a lot of history to the song. He sang it in 1935. He sang it with his now-deceased sister. He has many layers of memory connecting him to God in a familiar way with that song. At first, the song was just a pretty song to Christina. She learned it. Around that same time, my wife's father was dying of cancer. The whole family went out to see him. On a Sunday night, our family and my wife's siblings and their families gathered to share words of encouragement. That night my father-in-law blessed each family member. Then we in turned blessed him, thanking him for his prayers and witness. My daughter Christina walked over to Grandpa and held his hand and sang "In the Sweet Bye and Bye." She sang it without instruments, without music. There wasn't a dry eye in the room. And all of us were encouraged in our walk with God and our connection to Grandpa.

My friend Steve Elzinga explains the power of such moments in his 2002 book, *The Secret to a Great Music Ministry*:

> That is what music does. It connects us, it communicates for us, and it joins us in emotional ways that would otherwise be awkward for most families. It allows us to say things to each other and God that we wouldn't otherwise have the emotional courage to say. It allows us to connect with our shared past without someone retelling all the shared past. It allows us to feel emotion at a level we might otherwise run away from.

*   *   *

147

Repetition: Making Time Each Day

In many ways, the biggest battle you must win in a home-discipleship family walk is the battle of repetition—actually starting and sustaining a regular time of home discipleship. This is the battle that makes you face all your walls and obstacles. For instance, if you have a child who doesn't want to sit still for family devotions, you will have to deal with that wall. Eventually either the child will win or the parents will win. Maybe you have a child who refuses to sing. Do you sing anyway, or do you quit? Maybe you have tried doing family devotions in the past and it worked for a while, but then it faltered. It can be very hard to start a new habit and even harder to start one you've dropped.

The battle for repetition is the battle for the very habits of your home—either you will determine your habits, or your habits will determine who you become. Is television a higher priority than doing family devotions? Are sports more important than practicing home discipleship? This is a battle that we cannot afford to lose. We must be realistic about what kinds of obstacles we will face at one point or another.

Many parents tell me they have problems because they did not begin these practices when their families were young. It is often difficult to introduce new habits in a family that is set in its ways. Getting your 16-year-old son to participate in memorizing Scripture when he has never done it before may be a challenging sell. Yet whatever age your children are at, there is room to do something. Start small and see how God rewards that.

Many parents fear practicing home discipleship because they have misconceptions of how much time it will take. The fact is that practicing home discipleship at the family level ordinarily does not take more than twenty minutes a day. If a family spent five minutes reading the Bible or doing a devotional, five minutes doing memorization, five minutes singing a song, and five minutes in prayer, that would be a workable schedule.

Sometimes it is hard to practice repeated home discipleship because there is marital or family discord. Maybe the father and mother are in disagreement about whether the family should even practice home discipleship. Or both might agree, but a strong-willed child seeks to sabotage the time together. I don't have a simple answer for overcoming these difficulties. The first step is to see the truth about where you are right now and start talking about how to make as many changes as are needed.

Many find it difficult to practice home discipleship because there is no time when everyone is actually together. You might have to make some serious changes in your schedule to accomplish this. I suggest tying home-discipleship practices to the conclusion of a meal. Family members could open the meal with a short prayer, and afterward they could read a manageable passage, memorize a verse, sing a song, and close in prayer. Eating and worshiping together is a tradition that stretches back centuries in many Christian families and has big benefits for walking together closely as a family. It doesn't have to be dinner; many home-discipleship families meet for breakfast. Some meet at 11:00 p.m. for ice cream, as that's the only time the older children will be home. This is another area in which your family will have to sit down and really negotiate. Maybe you will start out meeting only once a week or twice a week. That's a place to begin. The most important thing is to do something.

Dealing with failure is a tough reality. Many who run into obstacles conclude that home discipleship does not work for them. The fact is that you may have some fundamental questions to ask yourself about being a parent and living up to that responsibility. Do you want to know the truth about your family? Do you want to deal with the hard questions that you have been avoiding for years? If you deny the truth that your family is struggling, do you think your family will someday just start practicing home discipleship on its own?

Some may say, "I am saved by grace, not works, and home discipleship feels like a truckload of works." Yes, you are saved by grace. You walk your familiar walk in grace. God loves you as a person if you don't practice home discipleship tonight. The question is: Do you believe that your family needs to intentionally practice walking with God together to keep from drifting? Are you going to hand over the spiritual life of your children completely to the church or to teachers or to a video series, or are you going to participate in it? Are you going to model for your children that sometimes the regular repetition of spiritual works allows us to see more clearly the grace in our lives?

Remember that Satan and his demons want to keep your family from meeting around God's Word and prayer. Your own sinful nature does not delight in handing your will and your time over to God. So pray for the strength to overcome any obstacle that holds you back. You will be in for major delights as you, by God's grace, overcome your family home-discipleship walls and begin to see the long-term benefits of a family walking with God.

The repeated aspect of doing something is what turns your discipleship walk and your familiar family walk into a family culture. If you practice your discipleship walk every once in a while, your familiar walk with God will suffer and your family will not really "sense" that walking with God is something that "we" do. The repetition area is something that takes effort. But if you keep it up, you will see the culture of your family change. You will see attitudes change. A new culture will emerge.

One tool that you can use is the *Christian Leaders Family Journal.* This journal actually keeps track of the home-discipleship practices of the whole family. The journal also encourages a weekly family meeting. At this meeting, you can gather once a week for a few moments and coordinate everyone's schedule. If you use the journal, the first month will tell you the truth about your current home-discipleship practices; then you will be able to pray about what those practices should become. The journal will also help you be very reproducible in your practices. That means that you can show your friends and neighbors your journal and talk about the difference it's making in your family. You can give them the gift of a journal of their own. It also means your children will be able to reproduce home discipleship in their families. (See Appendix B to see details of what is in the journal as well as how you can order one.)

Sometimes I think that we live in an age unique from any other. Technology seems to have changed the world so much. But the human heart is no different; it has always put up walls and barriers to deeper connections to God and family. Often I read great Christian leaders from other ages who observe problems that seem downright modern in their relevance. Presbyterian minister James W. Alexander recognized many walls that confronted his New York congregation. He wrote in *Family Worship*:

> Look at the living tide which rolls every morning down such a thoroughfare as Broadway! A stranger might be forgiven if he supposed that the life of each breathless banker, merchant, or clerk, depended on his reaching the commercial latitudes within a certain minute. But how many of these have prayed with their families? Some, we rejoice to believe; but the mass have no time for anything but the world. Unless men will lose their own souls, and jeopardy the souls of their children, they must take time for God. And the more busy, exhausting, and absorbing any man's days are, the more does he need the deliberate abstraction of a quiet devotional hour, such as that of Family-Worship.

What Alexander acknowledged in 1847 we acknowledge in the 21st century. We need the "deliberate abstraction" of home discipleship to keep the hearts of our family members focused on Christ!

Chapter 8

Connection Four:
Likeminded Fellowships

THE BOOK of Acts in the New Testament is a book about the early spontaneous spread of Christianity. The spread is the work of the Holy Spirit. You can't read Acts and not see the role that like-minded believers banding together had in setting up churches. In Acts you see powerful leaders like Peter, John, Paul, Stephen, Barnabas, Apollos, Philip, Mark, and Silas, not to mention the other disciples and many other leaders God raised up. These leaders founded fellowships and churches wherever they went. In those days, ordinary and unschooled men like the disciples who had been with Jesus were able to share their walk with others. In those days, extraordinary and trained men like Paul and Apollos who had been with Jesus were able to share their walk with others. The leaders in the book of Acts did not have sound systems; they did not do advertising; they did not have a special Easter service. This group of leaders simply walked with the Lord, and they were commanded to spread the good news that anyone could walk with the Lord, both Jew and Gentile. The risen Messiah will relate to anyone who will believe and acknowledge Christ as Lord.

I have been a church planter since graduating from Calvin

Seminary in 1987. My dream has been to see the church spread like it did in the book of Acts. I have read Acts over and over again. I have studied what other writers and theologians have observed about what God did in the book of Acts. I have brought my own experiences in planting four churches and helping hundreds of leaders plant churches into the mix in my study of Acts. All my study brings me back to the man who tried to get me to join Amway. He was a guy who walked the Amway walk, and he invited me and my family to join him in that walk. He told us that the Amway path was difficult but that I did not have to worry. Other leaders would be able to help me lead my family. In fact, groups (or fellowships) had formed that had the same mission to walk the Amway path of product use and to share that path with others. The man said that I would be mentored (discipled, so to speak) in how to be an effective leader. As an effective leader, I would sponsor others onto the Amway path. I would become a great leader both as I followed those who had gone before me and as I served and mentored those who would join Amway.

In being mentored by the cofounder of Amway, Rich DeVos, I clearly understand why Amway has spread to millions of distributors throughout the globe. The really amazing thing about Amway is that, for the most part, people who join are motivated by something as simple as a dream. Another significant thing about Amway is that Amway understands the power of family-like connections. Multilevel marketing is really the family tree applied to a business model. The sponsors are the parents. The newly sponsored recruits are the children. The goal of the parents is to get their children to grow up and become parents themselves. An effective sponsor spends focused time with his distributors, just as an effective parent spends focused time training his children.

What does all this have to do with the book of Acts? Jesus

has spent three years training (or sponsoring) his small group of disciples. He spent time with them, invested in them, and now he is sending them out to lead others in following God's way. Their mission is not to train every single person on earth but to equip their own trainees to train others as well. They are to create "generations" of spiritual leaders. In Amway they call those downlines. Each of us today who believes in Christ is part of a downline from one of the original disciples, trained by Christ himself. They have passed on a reproducible walk with God.

The apostle Paul was also directly sponsored by Christ on the road to Damascus; he did not meet Christ physically, but Jesus spoke to him directly and charged him with spreading the gospel. Paul even called himself one who was abnormally born (1 Corinthians 15:8). Paul also sponsored many leaders. He sponsored Gentiles like Timothy and Silas. These downlines stretch even to this day, as leaders sponsor or mentor new Christians. Billions have been led into a walk with Christ from Paul's original efforts. Many more will be led and mentored before Christ comes again.

So from these original leaders, fellowships were formed and new Christian leaders were identified. It is interesting to note that these leaders ministered to individuals, couples, and families. The new groups that were formed included individuals (such as the Ethiopian eunuch of Acts 8:27), couples (like Priscilla and Aquila of Acts 18:2), and families (Acts 11:14; 16:15; 16:31; 18:8). Christianity was for men, women, and children alike (Acts 2:39).

The Christian church consisted of fellowships that were multigenerational and multiethnic. Christianity grew as Christian leaders found others to become followers of Christ's Way and to join fellowships of like-minded believers who supported their walks with God. They mentored these followers to be leaders of their home and of others. If they had a household, they were to be the leaders of their children to make them in turn leaders of their children into Christ's Way. In fact, the walk in their family was a powerful testimony to Christ. I love the part in Acts where Paul stopped in at Philip's house. Philip's witness was clearly seen in his daughters, who were on fire for the Lord and were telling others about Jesus (Acts 21:8-9).

If Christian followers did not have a household, they spread the message to anyone who would listen. Paul was unmarried as he spread the gospel to individuals, couples, and families. The single Ethiopian eunuch formed fellowships. These groups formed churches. Tradition holds that the Ethiopian eunuch spread Christianity into Ethiopia. To this day, the Ethiopian believers acknowledge this one man as the father of Christianity in Ethiopia.

Like-minded Fellowships Today

I remember a phrase that was repeated over and over again in the late 1980s: "Find a need and fill it." The church-growth movement was built on phrases like this. Church-growth guru Rick Warren wrote *The Purpose-Driven Church* and *The Purpose-Driven Life*; both books emphasize programs that are tailor-made to fill the specific needs of people in their quest for God. If you go to Rick Warren's church, you will be able to join hundreds of different small groups. Each of these fellowships has a different purpose. In addition to Rick Warren's contributions, the Alpha Course, Willow Creek's New Community, and hundreds of individual churches have taken small groups and made them very effective in their purposes.

There seem to be certain characteristics that are common in most small groups or fellowships today. They are:

- based on individuals' needs

- often need-based evangelistic
- based on having a trained leader or a curriculum
- where "real church" happens, as many participants will tell you about their small group or fellowship
- a place to meet new friends, and a support system for building the relationship network in a local church

The strengths of modern small groups or fellowships are that they reach a lot of different types of people, can make up for the impersonal larger events of worship, and provide a place where someone can get a specific need met.

The modern small group can reach very diverse people and get them together. Take the Alpha Course, which is very popular today. This course provides a very safe atmosphere to talk about spiritual things in the context of meeting in small groups. Half the fun is meeting new people and eating together. The topics, Bible verses, and studies are very evangelistic.

Many of the small groups are programs designed to meet very specific needs. Many churches form groups that deal with recovery issues—from alcohol or drug addictions to overcoming specific hurts in your life from your past. These fellowships can be of great benefit to people who have had trouble getting their lives on track.

The Spiritual Foster Care System

Historically, the Sunday school movement developed more than a century ago to reach unchurched children. Churched children were taught at home in a home-discipleship environment. Over the years, and especially since WWII, the Sunday school small-group programs have been the location that replaced the home as the discipleship environment for passing on the faith to the next generation. You can especially see this shift as evidenced in church architecture. If you visit a church building built before 1900, you'll notice that there are not a lot of Sunday school rooms. The fact was they did not need them. Most discipleship happened in the home, supported by the church.

A similar kind of trend is emerging in the small group system; it is becoming a spiritual foster care system. This is certainly not the intended result of starting these need-based small-group fellowships, whether they are education programs like Sunday school or relational small groups. The framers of the Sunday school movement did not intend that Sunday school would replace the family as the primary discipleship tool for passing the faith on to the next generation. They could not have imagined that the family would break down to the point that Christian families would not engage in daily family instruction and worship.

It is understandable that the role of the church would increase as the family weakened. The leaders of the church see the weakness of the family. The leaders see that the family is having trouble discipling their children to walk with God. The church's answer is to create specific programs for different ages and interests. We make these programs entertaining and very relevant. We develop curriculum tailored for different age groups. We treat the children as individuals, apart from their siblings or parents. In a sense, the church becomes the spiritual foster care provider for the children.

Spiritual foster care alleviates the immediate problem (that children are not being mentored) but does little to address the root cause of the weakness of the family. In fact it actually makes the family weaker by: 1) eliminating the expectation that parents should train their own children in the Lord, 2) giving each member of the family his or her own leaders to look up to, topics of study, favorite songs, and developing memories, none of which are shared by the family as a whole, and 3) tapping the family for the money and often the time and skill to pay for and organize a spiritual foster care system. The expense associated with hiring more paid staff to plan, organize, and implement the programs makes it such that only the larger churches have the necessary resources to do spiritual foster care well. We see the proliferation of specialized church staff increasing all over North America, often drawing parents away from their families to do the teaching and work. Despite good intentions by all involved, families continue to get weaker.

The small-group movement is suffering from many of these same disasters in an effort to reach individuals at a place where they are already interested and comfortable.

An "entertain me" mentality has been planted in the hearts and minds of those attending American churches. When we form programs and groups that set an expectation that the church is going to entertain you or meet all your needs, children and adults grow to expect their Christianity to be served to them on a silver platter. The group or program attendee becomes more passive. Instead of taking personal responsibility to grow in a walk with God, many want the church to do it for them.

A competitive mindset develops that ultimately devalues the church and its leaders. One church's program is compared with another church's program. Many families find that one kid likes a program in one church and not in another one. Church programs are evaluated the way television programs are evaluated. You turn one on and turn another one off.

The church culture doesn't lend itself to foster care naturally. The church is a voluntary organization. People participate and volunteer hours toward the advancement of the kingdom of God. The spiritual foster care programs put volunteerism out of balance. I have seen church members try to help everybody else's children and lose their own.

The spiritual foster care system makes families too busy to

actually spend time as a family where home discipleship can thrive. I kept thinking of that when I visited Rick Warrren's church and when I've read his books. His books talk about forming groups to encourage Bible reading and prayer. I agree with that. But then he wants a commitment to volunteerism in various ministries without ensuring the development of a support system by which a person actually succeeds at Bible reading and prayer.

The fragmentation of the family is another unintended result of the spiritual foster care system. This fragmentation occurs at many levels. In many churches, the children do not sit in the service with their parents. The children have a program especially designed for them. The church service is designed especially for the adults. If the church ministry is effective, the children learn to like different things than the adults do. The children do not learn how to sit in services, and they learn to expect immediate gratification in their church relationship.

The lack of appropriate loyalty of the individual to his or her family is another unintended result; in the spiritual foster care system, the church leaders form special relationships with the children. Since spiritual questions guide and steer the direction of a person or young person, the advice given to a child may be in conflict with the spiritual direction of the family. What makes this difficult to gauge is the fact that in some cases the family has no spiritual direction. Then the foster care environment seems right. But in families that have a healthy balance, the spiritual foster care system can actually cause conflict or confusion. An example of this can be seen in many youth programs: The youth pastor is "cool," the parents stodgy and old-fashioned. The youth pastor expects loyalties to him that are in conflict with the direction set forth by the parents.

Another unintended result of the spiritual foster care structure is the burnout of leaders. Because the foster care system takes a vast quantity of human resources to run effectively, many leaders and pastors burn out trying to pull it together. To do spiritual foster care effectively, it takes great amounts of time and emotional energy. This happens because we are not equipping people to be leaders of others but are trying to do all the leading as a handful of experts.

The spiritual foster care mentality is especially attractive in North America, where it's considered OK to outsource anything we're not good at; efficiency is key. The pastor is so much better at gleaning insights than we are, so we pay him to do our walk with God and catch the highlight reel. So many individuals want the church to do more programs and events to help their broken lives instead of taking personal responsibility to walk with God.

I've held many seminars for pastors and their spouses concerning spiritual foster care programs, and those involved in the struggle are always quick to see that what they're working at is failing. Many ministers would weep and say, "I'm tired," or "Thank you for helping me put words to what I have seen." Then the question would come: "What do we do to change this?"

Home-Discipleship Fellowships

The good news is that we can change the system. There is a role that small groups can take in truly supporting and recognizing individuals, couples, and families and contributing positively to their familiar and intentional walks with God.

As you may have guessed from my critique of spiritual foster care, what needs to be changed is 1) involving each person in a family and in the church in the same spiritual practice, so across the board each person relates to what all the others are doing. We each need to be involved in playing the same "game," so to speak, so we can cheer each other on, share tips with each other, and reward one another. Breaking down the Christian life to its most basic, most thrilling core is the practice of talking and listening with God repeatedly. Everyone from the youngest child to the oldest senior can do this, from the newest Christian to the respected leader. Small groups should be organized not around gender, age, level of education, neighborhood, or need, but should be changed to 2) revolve around who is succeeding best at walking with God personally, walking with God in a marriage context, leading one's family in a walk with God, and helping other families walk with God.

In other words, the leaders emerge naturally from those whom God has gifted to help others in a spiritual walk. This might be a different group of people from those who have a lot of education or know of a good curriculum. This might be a different group than you'd get when asking for volunteers or even paid positions. These are not necessarily the people who are good at building a program from the ground up; what they're good at is being faithful in talking and listening to God, and they have a heart for passing that on to others. Making the switch could involve many bruised egos. But the power of Christianity isn't in running lots of great mini-programs. It is the single fundamental "game" of talking and listening to God that all Christians should be playing. We need to tap the leaders who play the game well and can inspire others to play.

Let's make this more concrete: Take baseball in America. Baseball has been considered our national pastime. In recent years, though, baseball has gone through some hard times. Take me, for instance. I grew up and played baseball. I played on the sandlot, in Little League, traveling league, and in high school. I loved going to baseball games to watch others play. I loved going to major league games. I imagined being good enough to be a major league player.

When I was first married back in the 1980s, I attended several major league games a year. Then my son was born. He grew up interested in soccer and golf. My sports world was no longer baseball. But I still went to games, and I took my son along. Then a crisis in my baseball walk occurred. The players walked off their job in 1994. I became disillusioned toward baseball. I was critical of the owners and the players. I no longer played the game in my own life, and my son was not playing the game in his life. I was not teaching the game to my daughters. My wife had no interest in baseball. And I was playing a different game, golf. My critical attitude intensified because I no longer cared as much about the game, because the game was not much of a culture in my family.

I have not been to a baseball game since 1994. I am open to go to one because it would likely bring me memories of my youth. But my family doesn't even know the rules of the game. They might attend a game as a human-interest endeavor, but they would not ask to go to a game. A few years ago, Jerry Reinsdorf, president of the Chicago White Sox, said that the future of baseball depends on getting kids to play baseball and not soccer. Players of the game will fill the stadiums.

Small groups need to be more like sandlot teams and Little League teams. The church service is the major-league event where professionals practice all the talking and listening to God; we get inspired by practiced prayers, the insightful Bible exposition, the beautiful singing. We cheer on others playing the game. But it doesn't mean as much to us unless we are involved in these practices in our own lives. Our small groups should not be about watching the game yet again but playing the game. Depending on our skill level, we find ourselves in high-school ball or the double-A club. Players of Christianity will fill the churches.

How does one advance in the game of talking and listening to God? You begin with taking time for simple prayer and Bible reading. Then you develop a habit of doing it every day. You involve others in your family in this habit. As you advance in the game, you will memorize Scripture and memorize songs. You'll maybe even sing these songs or hymns in parts. You'll look for mentors to help you advance in your play. You'll begin to play sandlot ball in a fellowship of others trying to get a family walk going. As you advance, you'll study the doctrines of Christianity. Soon you'll use your specific gifts in helping others play the game. You'll become a recruiter for the game. People will ask you about the fun you are having playing this game. You'll show them much of the game by your familiar walk with Christ. You or another leader can introduce them into their own familiar walk with Christ, if they have never started a relationship with God. And you will know how to get them to intentionally advance in the game. You can coach them. You will invite them to fellowships of those who want to play. You'll be leading your own sandlot league.

Setting Up Intentional Home-Discipleship Groups

If you want to set up fellowships that support your home-discipleship walk, you must first examine the habits of your current familiar and intentional fellowship walk and determine what needs changing. The familiar fellowship walk is something you may not even notice. This is the "walk with others" part of your life.

In the past, when people tended to live their whole lives in one location, the extended family was the primary familiar fellowship. The extended family included grandparents and uncles and aunts. In a Christian culture, extended households walked and talked their faith in shared community. I remember Sundays in the 1970s. After church, the relatives would all come to my house for coffee after church. Much of the discussion concerned the sermon. Some of the discussion concerned members

164

of the family and their choices in life. If someone got out of line, family peer pressure would speak volumes to the wayward one. In the case of the extended family, it can be that the familiar walk and the intentional home-discipleship walk are hardly distinguished.

My parents have an apartment in our home. We eat one meal together. We practice home discipleship with Grandpa and Grandma. We go to the same church, and participate in many things together. We have a familiar walk with each other. Many times my dad or mom will mentor my wife and me or our five children. Intentional discipleship occurs, but it is often not noticed. The most intentional aspect was to set it up that my parents actually live with us. The fact is, we have a home-discipleship-support fellowship group for our family right at home.

Today, most people experience a familiar fellowship walk with their friends. It is very interesting to see how people relate in peer groups. That relationship with peer groups will even include how someone dresses and how someone talks. The fact is that there can be fellowship-familiar-walk drift. Peer pressure can bring you down. Some groups are just not good for your walk. On the other hand, if your friends are believers who love the home-discipleship game, together you will encourage each other to walk closely with God. We have heard about negative peer pressure; there also is something called positive peer pressure. When you are with people who encourage you to walk with the Lord, your walk will rise to higher heights.

If you want to change your familiar walk with your friends, you will first have to make strategic changes in your intentional fellowship walk. It won't change much to ask your friends just once a month how their walk is going; take steps toward setting up a home-discipleship fellowship that supports the playing of the spiritual-walk game in your homes. To some you will be introducing "sandlot" home discipleship; to others you will be supporting their desire to practice home discipleship. This probably won't happen overnight, but if you already have a strong personal walk, marriage walk, and family walk, chances are that you'll have a lot to share with others you want to get on board. If you don't have a strong walk in your home, don't wait until you do to start a support network; chances are you need it now more than ever. Just share your vision for what your families could do if they support one another. The basic steps toward developing a fellowship ministry that supports home discipleship are these:

Step One: Finalize the Walking Plan for your Own Household

In the previous chapters, you were encouraged to try various ideas for home discipleship. When you recruit someone to join a home-discipleship small group, you will want to show exactly what habits you plan to work on together. What reading track are you following? What prayer guide do you use? What hymns are you singing?

Step Two: Decide What Type of Fellowship You Will Form or Participate In

One really effective way to support home discipleship is through the practice of hospitality. At our home-discipleship church, we encourage families to invite each other over for meals and fellowship. After the meal, the gathering families meet to read the Bible passage of the day and to recite Bible passages each family is working on. Then the gathered families may share a song or hymn or two. At the hospitality level, the home-discipleship pattern will look very similar to what the families practice in their homes. This practice informally encourages families to keep up their home discipleship. Try forming a hospitality group that is intentional about inviting newcomers to the church, rather than just working on your own. You will need encouragement to keep going.

A second suggestion is to attach home discipleship to a pre-existing group or meeting that you are already a part of. Maybe you are on a building committee at your church. Maybe you are gathering with other Christian farmers at a coffee shop once a week. Maybe you are in a sewing club. Maybe you are holding a birthday party for a child or a Christmas gathering. Maybe you are going out with friends to a restaurant. Practice some form of home discipleship. Sometimes it may only be a prayer. If you take a pocket Bible with you to a restaurant, why not read some Scripture while you wait for your food? At any church gathering, commit the meeting to God and open with discipleship.

A third excellent option is to hold a once-a-month hymn sing and potluck for those in your church or circle of influence who are practicing home discipleship. You might start with two or three other families, and as more people are interested, you can expand. A meeting like this might turn into a new church plant, the way Family of Faith started when my wife and I began a hymn sing. Maybe it will just stay a hymn sing. It still helps to encourage families in their personal, marriage, and family walks knowing that there is a "sandlot" to show off the skills they learned throughout the week in their backyards. These groups also benefit from ample opportunities for their young people to meet for courtship purposes. Here is an agenda for a typical hymn sing:

- Potluck
- Opening Prayer
- Hymn
- Families Recite Memorized Passages
- Hymn
- Families Recite Memorized Passages
- Hymn

- Families Recite Memorized Passages
- New Hymn of the Month
- Families Recite Memorized Passages
- Current Hymn of the Month
- Closing Remarks and Prayer

My fourth suggestion is to hold weekly or bi-weekly meetings with several other families who are practicing home discipleship. These gatherings will be simliar to a typical church small group or Bible study, insofar as a group of families meets regularly to dig into the Scriptures together. But unlike most such groups, the children stay with their parents and participate. Unlike most groups, the families will have read and discussed the Scriptures on their own before coming to the group and sharing what they've learned. Other aspects of home discipleship will be recognized, rewarded, and reinforced in these meetings. Here is a typical meeting agenda for a 45- to 90-minute gathering:

- Opening Prayer
- Previous Week's Bible Review: The group will have chosen a Bible-reading path. Someone will prepare questions from the Bible reading for families to answer. Special attention should be paid to picking both hard questions and easy questions to allow people of all ages to participate.
- Family Recognition Time: Many of these groups set reward levels in the practice of home discipleship. The Smith family, for instance, sets a goal to practice home discipleship for twenty-one days in a row. They announce their success, and everyone claps and praises God for that new discipline. This is very effective in jumpstarting intentional home-discipleship practices.
- Worship: Many groups are keeping hymn singing alive. If you pick a hymn of the month, families could memorize that hymn at home all month. You can even learn this

hymn in parts. There are great resources available to learn parts even if you do not have a piano player at home. (See Appendix A to learn about the *Christian Leaders Home Discipleship Hymnbook* and CD resources.)

- Family Recitation Time: Participating families recite together the Bible passages the family has memorized.
- Bible Study: This study is selected from the seven passages that the families had read in their home during the week. Share with each other interesting insights or discussions you had that week from your readings.
- Prayer Time: Ask for prayer requests and close your meeting with prayer.

Step Three: Be on the Lookout for People to Mentor You

Finding mentors is an important step of practicing home discipleship at the fellowship level. When I was planting my first church back in 1987, God called Marty and Ruth Ozinga to help my wife and me and another young couple plant a new church. Marty and Ruth were about ten years older than we were. They had an excellent home-discipleship walk with God, and they were the parents of six boys. Ruth Ozinga was a powerful mentor to my wife, modeling both a godly familiar and intentional walk. Marty modeled a godly walk with godly leadership to me as a young pastor. One of the things that they challenged us to do was begin marriage devotions. This practice has stuck with us now for almost twenty years. When you find a mentor and are open to learning from the mentor, you have created a powerful small group of discipleship training.

I have been blessed with many excellent mentors. While I was a pre-seminarian, Rev. Marvin Heyboer spent hours mentoring me in being a pastor who was a spiritually alive leader, not a rent-a-pastor. Pam and I were mentored by Dr. Carl George and his wife, Grace, in many practical ways toward becoming effective fellowship leaders.

Steve and Marie Elzinga have been mentors and godly peers in our lives. Steve and I partnered for more than ten years to help church planters and lay people establish patterns of talking and listening to God daily. Steve has influenced me in ways that forced me to grow as a leader. It was in my partnership with Steve that the paradigm of the seven connections came to light. Steve and I had been talking and reflecting on discipleship for years. One day, we were taking a walk, and Steve ran by me the framework of the seven connections. Up to that point, we were seeing pieces of the puzzle; he saw how they fit together.

My wife and I started home schooling in 1994. This was a major shift for us. God raised up Jim and Greta De Korne to show us how home schooling worked. Since that time, we have been to conferences and other support gatherings. Michael and Vicki Farris were a tremendous encouragement to us when we met for three days in Florida. In fact, it was Michael who strongly encouraged me to write this book.

Other mentors and godly peers in our lives are our co-pastor and his wife at Family of Faith Church, Dave and Wendy Feddes. Dave has been the radio minister of the Back to God Hour. Though he is one of the most intelligent men I know, he is also humble, articulate and teachable. Wendy has been an excellent mentor and peer to my wife and children.

I could mention many more mentors and like-minded peers, such as the elders of our church and of previous churches I served. Other pastors, teachers, and leaders have made an impact. I have had some mentors from the business world. Godly mentors are everywhere if you will look for them. The act of finding a mentor is an intentional act of home discipleship.

Where do you begin the process of finding a mentor? I started in my own family. I am the youngest of four. I take the encouragement of my parents and older brothers and sister very seriously. You may also find mentorship possibilities with your pastor or with elders in your church.

The Bible is full of passages that speak to the importance of mentorship. Notice the mentor relationship of the apostles and the first leaders of the church in the book of Acts and Paul's epistles. Notice the generational mentorship verse telling the older women to mentor the younger ones and the older men to mentor the younger men (Titus 2:3-10).

Observe the walk of others. When you see someone who has a piece of the puzzle, ask that person to be your mentor. You will be surprised by the response you'll get. When I asked Rich DeVos to mentor me, I was in shock that he responded "yes" within 24 hours.

Find more than one mentor. No one person knows everything you need to know. If you're a married couple and you see another husband and wife who impress you with their relationship together, set up an appointment to talk to them. Ask them how they grow in their love with each other. Ask them about their spiritual walk with God and any other questions you have. Find family mentors. If you see a family that has it together, ask them how they do it! Be teachable and open to being in a home-discipleship network of friends and leaders who love the Lord.

Remember one important thing about finding mentors. Mentors are not perfect. They too are saved by grace yet are still human. They might not always give you perfect advice. Always test what your mentors say in accordance with God's Word. A godly Christian mentor would not ask you to do otherwise. The apostle Paul actually complimented the Bereans in the book of Acts because they checked the Scriptures to see if his mentorship conformed to the Word of God.

Now the Bereans were of more noble character than the Thessalonians, for they received the message with great eagerness and examined the Scriptures every day to see if what Paul said was true. (Acts 17:11)

A godly mentor leads in his or her walk with Christ; this leader does not have a control complex.

Remember always to treat parents, elders, pastors, leaders, employers, community leaders, and mentors with respect, because you are being watched by others who look up to you. If you complain about your parents and your pastor, if you complain about those over you, including your boss, you will model disrespect to those who are watching you. If you show those who look up to you that you will follow godly leadership, you will mentor others to follow godly leadership. How you treat your own parents is how your children will treat you.

> Show proper respect to everyone: Love the brotherhood of believers, fear God, honor the king. (1 Peter 2:17)

Develop an attitude that is open to others' leadership in your life. So many Christians suffer from an unteachable spirit. You can't become a great leader until you are first a great follower. Follow Christ in your familiar walk and your discipleship walk, and you will receive the role of the Christian leader in your life.

Step Four: Recruiting Others to Play

Your calling is to become a leader of others into a walk with Christ. Your calling is to introduce the "game" of talking and listening to God repeatedly. That is what the great commission challenges us to do. We are not to be only disciples. We are to reproduce discipleship with those God has placed in our lives. Of course, this starts in our own homes, in our own marriages, and in our own families. But those who are Christ's disciples are to lead others to Christ and to walk with him and serve him. Recruiting and leading others to walk with Christ is the call of every Christian and especially every Christian leader.

> Then Jesus came to them and said, "All authority in heaven and
> on earth has been given to me. Therefore go and make disciples
> of all nations, baptizing them in the name of the Father and of
> the Son and of the Holy Spirit, and teaching them to obey every-
> thing I have commanded you. And surely I am with you always,
> to the very end of the age." (Matthew 28:18-20)

Make a list of people you think need to hear about a reproducible home-discipleship walk. Go to your address book and
ask this question about every one of your personal contacts.
Does this person need to hear about a home-discipleship walk?
Write down the names of at least three people and commit to
pray for each one you wrote down. Then invite their families over
to your house and share with them your home-discipleship
practices. If some of your friends are interested in what you are
doing, you might consider starting a fellowship group that supports home discipleship. If you attend a home-discipleship
church or some other home-discipleship event, ask your friends
to come and find out more about home discipleship.

The Dangers of Expecting Too Much
of Fellowship-Sized Groups

Let me express a word of caution about developing too much of
an attachment to home-discipleship fellowship groups.
Especially if you are not part of a home-discipleship church,
these groups can be very fulfilling as they meet a deep spiritual
need to participate in something larger than ourselves, to be
recognized for our efforts, and to experience the positive peer
pressure of a God-seeking culture. There is a temptation to
think of this small group of people as your "real church," and the
larger gatherings of hundreds on Sunday as something less

worthwhile. There is a danger in reducing your need for others to such a small circle and neglecting the biblical and legitimate role of the church and the kingdom in supporting your walk with God. These small fellowships are often very meaningful at the beginning, but they can transform to unhealthy spiritual environments when too much weight is placed on them. Some in Christian home-schooling circles have been promoting home discipleship and suggesting that the optimal church size be fifty to sixty people. This type of thinking will damage Christ's church. Here are some of the dangers I see in placing church-level demands on the structure of fellowship groups:

Sometimes a fellowship becomes almost too close. Many times families who spend too much time together start crossing appropriate boundaries. Or familiarity breeds contempt, so to speak, and the families know so much about each other that they start making dangerous evaluations of each other. Sometimes a strong male or female in the mix will start micromanaging other families to fix their problems. I do not want to say that this always happens, but it often does. The close families cannot maintain this "closeness," and the fellowship breaks apart with certain families or individuals experiencing hurt.

If you reduce the optimum size of church to the fellowship level, you will hurt the historical culture of "church." Some Christian leaders have recently advocated that the perfect church size should be less than sixty. They have strong anecdotal evidence to support their views: When families gather for weekly Bible study, prayer, and singing, it creates a very strong environment for accountability. There is such strength in holding each other accountable. There is such an enthusiasm for seeing leaders read the Bible and pray. For some, this is like a rediscovery of the Reformation's tenet of the "priesthood of all believers." There is certainly a short-term benefit of advancing some like-minded beliefs and theology. It is no wonder why certain leaders have made fellowships all the church they perceive they need.

The reasons these types of reductions hurt the culture of the church is manifold. It is not biblical to suggest that there is an optimal church size. While it is true that some churches will be small because of various factors, the Bible never prescribes a church size. In the book of Acts, we see both a fellowship size and a larger gathering of believers in a city. If we look at the seven churches in Revelation, some of those churches were small and some were large. Church sizes are set by the work of the Holy Spirit.

If you advocate fellowship-sized local gatherings as "church," you will also hurt the development of leadership in the Christian movement. As there is usually no central leader in a fellowship, with many of the responsibilities shared, our brightest and best young leaders will not aspire to do full-time work in the church. They often put one foot in the church and one foot in the work-force, depleting our churches of those who work solely at ensuring its health. In addition, smaller fellowships do not lend themselves to situations where a minister can receive a necessary wage so that his wife will be able to stay home to raise godly children. It is already a sad situation the way many churches pay their pastors. Many pastors' wives have been forced to work outside the home. I have heard very sad stories of many pastors who live at or below poverty level. Many church boards need to repent of allowing their pastors to be so poorly paid. If we want our brightest and best to aspire to the ministry, we had better be willing to honor them with a wage by which they will be able to provide for their families.

If you advocate fellowship-sized local gatherings as "church," the environment will not be conducive for our young people to study theology. The study of theology is very important for keeping our Christian culture from drifting into dangerous waters.

While I acknowledge that some seminaries or Bible schools have been the reason for drifting, it is also the case that excellent institutions of learning have equipped our Christian leaders with a biblical and theological foundation that have brought us godly leaders like Billy Graham, R.C. Sproul, and James W. Alexander. Returning to the baseball illustration: If we will want some big-league hitters, we need to have a culture that supports the development of these hitters.

If you advocate fellowship-size local gatherings as "church," you will also hurt the next generation's quest to find like-minded spouses. Today more than ever, young Christians are having a hard time finding each other. The church has always been a place where young Christian leaders found each other. The fact is that we need large gatherings to meet the courtship needs of our younger Christians. In home-schooling circles, of which I am a part, this need cannot be overstated. So many Christian home-schooling families are not hanging around with enough like-minded families to see courtship flourish. Many home schoolers have gathered in small fellowships, and the pool of like-minded home-discipleship families is too small. Though parents tell their children that they should be patient, the fact is that the pool is too small! At our home-discipleship church, we have fifty young Christians whose families practice home discipleship. Our church has many courtships, and we anticipate many more.

Home-discipleship fellowship groups are very important, despite these cautions. We need these small-size groupings as crucial infrastructure in building a home-discipleship culture. The accountability, encouragement, mentorship, and growth that happen in fellowship groups are very important for the growth of a healthy Christian culture.

Chapter 9

Connection Five:
The Church Connection

HARRY AND his wife, Linda, had not been to church since they were children. Harry attended the community church on special holidays. Linda went to a United Methodist church occasionally. Her dad stopped attending when she was nine; he quit because of a disagreement about a building project. Linda's whole family stopped attending church as well. Now that Harry and Linda have children, they have been thinking about connecting to a church again. They noticed that their 17-year-old boy, Sean, has been lying. They found drugs in his room, and he told Harry and Linda that the drugs belonged to his friend Tommy. They notice that their 15-year-old daughter, Sam, wants to wear suggestive and provocative clothes. She has already had two boyfriends. Sean and Sam constantly talk back to their parents. Harry and Linda also have a 12-year-old named Caitlin. She is watching her older two siblings.

Both Harry and Linda were raised in homes where pastors were just barely respected and church was considered boring. Though they were raised marginally under the influence of church, the Bible was not read in their homes, nor was God honored as a central character. Therefore, it was hard to pay attention to the messages since the Bible seemed remote and foreign. Messages were boring mainly because Harry and Linda had no idea what the minister was talking about. It was difficult to enjoy the hymns when their families did not sing hymns at home.

Harry and Linda started to talk about their situation. Linda remembered attending Sunday school. She remembered that they taught that you shouldn't lie. Harry was amenable enough to the concept of a "God" that he agreed to start thinking about bringing the children to church. They had already tried Ritalin; what harm could it do to try church? Around that time, a flyer came in the mail from a local community church. The flyer interested them. It said, "People are not against God ...they are against boredom. Come to our Community Church, a boredom-buster ministry!"

Harry and Linda laughed at the advertisement. They recalled their memories of church. They read on. The flyer introduced them to a ministry team that promised to reach them where they were at. They read about a message series that promised to bring their family back together. They read that the music was going to be contemporary and not traditional. This all sounded interesting. The flyer also promised that they would not have to sign anything or give anything. All they had to do was soak it in. The mailing also promoted a big event. A sports celebrity was going to tell what God had done in his life.

Harry and Linda decided to pitch the idea to the children. The children agreed to go but promised to go only once to hear what Mr. Baseball had to say.

Sunday morning came. Harry and Linda felt pretty good about themselves. They arrived at church with their three kids in tow a full three minutes early. They actually got a seat in the last row. "Perfect," thought Linda. "We can leave before anyone tries to make us sign up for anything." The service was upbeat. The message was positive and practical. The music sounded like the music the kids listened to on their iPods. The drama was moving. The children did not seem too turned off. The family left immediately. But they did come back the next week. In fact, they returned again and again.

After attending the community church for four years, Harry and Linda are generally happy with the role of church in their lives while they are struggling through the teen years of their children. Church has done the following for Harry and Linda:

- The services have often given them great comfort. The message of grace helped them cope with the mistakes they made with Sean. The support groups help Linda especially deal with the truth of Sean's drug addiction. They remain hopeful that Sean will still be moved by one of the positive messages from the church. They insist that Sean attend services with them as long as he lives at home. Sean is working odd jobs. Harry and Linda are hoping the church-sponsored job fair will give Sean a new opportunity.

- The youth group connected with this church has brought some mixed results. They determined to take the good with the bad. Their daughter Sam unfortunately continued in her boy-crazy ways. Sam continued to dress provoca-tively, and when she was seventeen, she caught the attention of another newcomer to the church. She and her boyfriend, Josh, were caught engaging in inappropriate sexual behavior. Still, Harry and Linda believe that her church involvement did restrain some of her actions. For that they are very thankful. Sam is now at college. Harry and Linda have no idea what is actually happening in her life, but they hope that the messages she heard at the community church will draw her back.

- Caitlin is now in the youth group. She really likes the 20-year-old guitar player, Nick, from the worship band. He loves classic rock. She loves it, too. Harry and Linda think there is no harm in this relationship so far.

- For Harry and Linda, church has been a good experience overall. They are happy with the pastor, Al. They have disagreed with some of his messages, and they wished he'd done more series on parenting teenagers when they needed insight. Harry and Linda liked how the church allowed them to come to God on their terms. When the church did the forty-day spiritual adventure, they sort of participated. Linda commented to her mother, "We never read so much Bible in our life." They were glad when the program finished but kept those thoughts to themselves. Church has become an important part of Harry and Linda's life. They never realized how pleasant the experience could be. The church provides them with all sorts of opportunities to meet other people. They met new friends, named Rick and Sue, in their small group, who have a very similar family situation. They have been great to talk to about the trials and tribulations of raising teens.

Harry and Linda and their children have plugged into a church that meets them where they are at. This is a church that allows them to grow with God at the pace they feel comfortable with. They are still not sure of their long-term involvement. They know that they will stay there as long as the kids are around. They will also continue as long as Pastor Al leads the church.

Pastor Al's Story

Recently, Pastor Al has thought about leaving the church; he is getting burned out. He and his wife planted the new church with the hopes of reaching the Harrys and Lindas of the neighborhood. The church's basic approach was to create a worship event that drew people to attend services. Then, once they attended, the staff's goal was to provide supporting small-group programs to reach different attendees in their specific needs.

Pastor Al could not complain about the growth of the church. Pastor Al has a heart to reach the unchurched; when he left seminary, he was full of ideas for drawing in those who remained outside church culture. He began with just a core group and now, after seven years, the church is filled with nearly 600 people. Along the way to that growth, Pastor Al has gone through cycles of burnout and renewal. He rejoiced that Harry and Linda had found a church home. He prayed for their children, that they would somehow take that next step toward Christ.

In Pastor Al's reflective moments, he has many concerns for his church and the long-term viability of this church-planting model:

- His attendees' walks are more shallow than deep. Even though he had a message series on reading the Bible and the church did the forty days of purpose, the people are not reading the Bible in their lives. He figures that less that 15% of his church reads the Bible regularly. He also feels like his church will not let him challenge them on reading the Bible. He reached them through an entertaining presentation. He set the expectation that they could just sit back and enjoy church. Now, to ask them to do home discipleship would be understood as "bait and switch." Pastor Al has seen that how you reach people is how they reproduce. If you reach them through an entertaining presentation and treat them as spectators, to get them to be players in their personal lives is very difficult.
- His attendees are very dependent on his leadership. An elder of his church raised the question, "What if you died in a car accident, Pastor? What would happen to the

church?" This was a big concern for Al. He knew that many of those he had reached felt their connection to God closely connected to their connection to him. He found it hard to find preachers to fill in for him when he was on vacation. He had to find the type of pastor that would be able at least to hit a single with this crowd, if not a grand slam. When he started the church, he figured that eventually he'd leave and the church would keep going for another hundred years. Now he doesn't want to think about what would happen if he were to leave.

- He feels the church is still fragile. Sometimes he will tell his wife, "I feel like our church could split with just one scandal." The loyalty of many in the church is conditional on how he keeps the services at the cutting edge. His people bore easily. He feels he has to be more and more interesting every week; if he isn't, his attendees will shop for a better deal. Often it seems he is part of the farm system for the even-larger mega-churches. When people did leave his church, most of them usually went to a bigger church that was even more on the cutting edge.

- He has also been concerned about what he calls the "weakening factor." It seems to him that Christianity as a *culture* is waning. He grew up with hymns and he liked them. Now the church sings the same forty contemporary songs over and over. He likes the contemporary songs, but to say goodbye to the hymns seems sad to him. Also sad is the fact that the great doctrines of the kingdom are not talked about at his church. People want to hear practical messages that directly affect their personal struggles. He figures that those doctrinal issues and traditional hymns are going to survive only at seminaries, not at churches. He has concluded there is nothing he can do about that.

- In his down moments, he wonders whether he is giving

people just an illusion of a walk with God when they show up on Sundays. He thinks that way because so many people's spiritual moods rise and fall by what they experienced on Sunday morning. They do not seem to have anything deeper that anchors them spiritually than whether or not he preached well that week. He feels that many are living spiritual lives vicariously through him. Other times he has the notion that he pre-chews the spiritual food for people to feed it to their hungry hearts.

• He has noticed that the larger the church has become, the more fragmented its families have become. They have one children's church for the preschooler, one for elementary, one for junior high, and one for high schoolers. Each of these services has a different purpose. This setup has bothered the home-schooling families in his church. Many have been leaving to do home church or find a home-discipleship church. He is beginning to see that his programs don't support family unity.

Pastor Al is also concerned about the model he used to plant this church. He is concerned that this model is not going to be the best to spread Christianity. He has many reasons:

• This church-planting model was very expensive. Pastor Al was able to raise enough capital to fund the latest sound systems, computer systems, staff, instruments, rented auditorium, advertising, and other expenses. But he has realized that much of the resources came from outside the congregation. The collections have not kept up with the pace of expenses. Pastor Al is concerned that this model is not very reproducible because it cost so much money to start one church.

• He has found that in some cases this church model actually contributes to making people unchurched. If you reach people in a highly emotional and entertaining presentation, and they stop coming to your church, the next church that reaches them most likely needs to be *more* entertaining. This is especially true for the young generation. The parents may like the blend of music that the community church delivers, but the children demand something more extreme. Pastor Al notices that the youth pastor has been putting together services that are even louder and more youth-culture oriented.

- He has also noticed the struggle of many pastors nearby who were trying to use this model but failed. It seems to Pastor Al that a model that resulted in a mega-church could be carried out by only very few churches. He is toying with the idea of video-feed churches. He has heard that this model might be able to help some churches grow.

- He also notices a new trend: People have become involved with many churches at the same time. Sometimes families with three children attend events at three different churches. Each person gets to choose his or her favorite. His church works hard to put on good programs to reach people but often finds itself in competition with nearby churches. It is as if more and more people pick and choose as spiritual consumers rather than as contributors to the growth of any one church.

Pastor Al is in no position to think much more about the pros and cons of the model of church he planted. He has messages to write and so much to do. He does conclude that if he could do it all over again, he would do some things differently. Besides, no one has shown him a better model. Sometime when he talks about making changes, he comes back to the same conclusion: "This is the best model available to contextualize Christianity in our day. It works for Rick Warren and Bill Hybels, and to some extent it has worked for me. Until God shows me something different, I'm sticking with what works."

Is there anything different out there? Doing things differently in a day when people seem to be leaving denominations and existing churches for more upbeat churches appears to be filled with risk. It seems like the church paradigm is heading in the direction of entertainment. Even though there are serious problems with the current church-growth model, before anyone is going to leave that model, there had better be something different that addresses many of the weakness and actually improves the impact of the church.

A New Reformation

Before I introduce the home-discipleship church model, I want to point out that the familiar and intentional distinction applies also at the church level. The familiar walk of the church connection very much relates to the spirit of the age. Contemporary music in churches is an example of this. The church did not hold a conference in the '60s and decide that the Beatles' style of music was going to overtake the sound of church worship. Worship music drifted in that direction because American music and culture drifted in that direction. The arts are becoming a major aspect of so many churches because our culture has come to value the visual. Movies and entertainment are a high priority in our culture. This drift has affected local churches by altering what they think they must do to communicate to the average person. One hundred years ago, people could sit and listen to a one-hour revival sermon and not be bored.

The local expression of church has always been subject to certain drifts. Some of the cultural drifts have been positive in their effect on the familiar walk of Christian culture. Other times the drifts have had a very negative effect. The apostle John wrote

God's judgment of a church that had drifted from a close walk with Christ:

> "To the angel of the church in Laodicea write: These are the words of the Amen, the faithful and true witness, the ruler of God's creation. I know your deeds, that you are neither cold nor hot. I wish you were either one or the other! So, because you are lukewarm—neither hot nor cold—I am about to spit you out of my mouth. You say, 'I am rich; I have acquired wealth and do not need a thing.' But you do not realize that you are wretched, pitiful, poor, blind and naked. I counsel you to buy from me gold refined in the fire, so you can become rich; and white clothes to wear, so you can cover your shameful nakedness; and salve to put on your eyes, so you can see." (Revelation 3:14-19)

Before the Reformation (1450 A.D.), the Christian church had drifted very heavily toward an exclusive emphasis on connection five—the institutional church. People's connection to God was almost synonymous with their connection to their local parish. Individuals did not read the Bible. In fact, the Bible was not available in the common languages; priests read the Bible in Latin.

In those days, the church was the center of art and culture. Some of the most beautiful religious art and stunning cathedrals were created in that era. And while the church as an institution was thriving, human hearts were waning. Church members were relegated to paying spectators whose impoverished souls were held in the balance of how their works measured up at their local parish.

The reformers saw that spiritual poverty. The church was winning; people were losing. Luther, Zwingli, Calvin, and others identified the familiar-walk drift. They corrected that drift by returning the Bible to its rightful place as the sole authority for Christian living. They realigned the church's role to support people in walking directly with God as spiritual players. The Reformation called the church back to a church walk that was more in concert with the Word of God. Ordinary men and women could have personal walks with God. The Reformation churches reintroduced family worship and put accountability systems in place to keep families from drifting in their walks with God. Worship services centered on preaching the Word again. The church did less in terms of mediating someone's spiritual walk, and the people did more.

I believe there are clear parallels between today's church culture and the drifting that occurred before the Reformation. Some things are very different. Some things are very similar. In western countries, most evangelical churches would still affirm the great theological truths uncovered by the Reformation. We hold firm the belief that salvation is a gift we receive through faith, not by earning it or paying for it. We look to the Bible as the cornerstone of spiritual truth. And because the Word of God is still being preached and respected, the Word will not return void. Lives will be changed. God will use Pastor Al to preach to Harry, Linda, and their kids.

There are, however, some places where the familiar walk of today's church is similar to the familiar walk of churches before the Reformation. Today, just like before the Reformation, people are spectators more than ever in their walks with God. Today the images are not hung on a wall or painted on a ceiling. The images are live in a church-produced drama. Today the images are on a screen. Often the message to the typical attendee of a church is that a spiritual walk is what happens at the worship service. Today we have built some impressive cathedrals again. Each major metropolitan area has several. Most evangelicals do not honor the pope in Rome, but they do give celebrity spiritual leaders higher esteem than the pope received before the Reformation. This is where we have drifted.

In order to change the church's familiar walk, it is necessary to change the intentional walk. That means asking why we do what we do. It means taking a hard look at our habits and practices and seeing where they are leading us. It means returning to the Bible, to the foundational mission for the church as set forth in the great commission:

> "Therefore go and make disciples of all nations, baptizing them in the name of the Father and of the Son and of the Holy Spirit, and teaching them to obey everything I have commanded you. And surely I am with you always, to the very end of the age." (Matthew 28:19-20)

The word "disciple" is the object of our task. The church is to make disciples of all nations. Disciples are not spectators. Disciples are active followers of Jesus. Churches are to preach the gospel in such a way as to support the success of believers in a growing obedient walk with God! The apostle Peter in his famous Pentecost message applied this truth to entire families:

> Peter replied, "Repent and be baptized, every one of you, in the name of Jesus Christ for the forgiveness of your sins. And you will receive the gift of the Holy Spirit. The promise is for you and your children and for all who are far off—for all whom the Lord our God will call." (Acts 2:38-39)

The church must look clearly at itself generation after generation until Christ comes again. Are we leading in such a way as to support reproducible evangelism and discipleship?

The Home-Discipleship Model of Church

A home-discipleship church seeks to build a home-discipleship culture in your home. You need to put habits and behaviors in place that ensure that an intentional walk with God is actually taking place. A home could be that of a single person, a married couple without children, or a family. Your home's success is a key priority of the church mission. This is a challenging task in a day where the home is fragmented by so many distractions. Many Christian individuals have wanted to have a home-discipleship walk with God, but, for many reasons, have struggled. Married couples have struggled with finding time to meet for marriage devotions. Christian families struggle to succeed at their home-discipleship practices. The fact is you need a church community that encourages, supports, and rewards a home-discipleship walk with God.

The Support of Preaching

The historical confessions of the faith stress the importance of preaching. Biblical preaching supports the development of your familiar walk with God. The Word of God preached at a worship service can—in a moment—change your life forever. If you have a hard heart toward God or a person, preaching can melt that heart into love. In many churches, preaching mainly ministers to the familiar walk; in a home-discipleship church, preaching ministers to both the familiar walk and the intentional walk.

In a home-discipleship setting, preaching also encourages us to open the Word of God on a regular basis in our homes. At a home-discipleship church, the preaching of the Word directly relates to what the congregation is reading in its home-discipleship devotions. Everyone in church is encouraged to read the same passages. The preaching supports the discussions that are happening about those passages in homes, at workplaces, over lunches, and across picket fences.

The preaching of the Word is part of the listening aspect of a talking-and-listening connection to God. When you open the Bible on your own, or when you read with your kids, or when a preacher expounds on a text in a full and deep sense so the meaning is made more clear and practical, in all cases the Word of God is being proclaimed. God is being heard. Linking these practices helps to reinforce and strengthen each element. If the only time you engage in the Word of God is on Sunday, you will handicap the impact of God's work in your life. The Sunday proclamation should be the *culmination* of the proclamations that have been going on all week in your home. When a family is opening the Word on a regular basis and talking about what is read, and then the preaching at church deepens the ongoing discussion, discipleship occurs in a very effective manner.

Church also provides a platform for increasing the success of home memorization habits in the lives of those in the church. Part of the worship service can be set aside for families to recite Bible passages. The congregation can recognize and applaud families for their efforts. This not only is of great encouragement to home-discipleship efforts, but the recitation of the Word is in itself a form of preaching.

The Support of the Sacraments

There are certain things a home especially needs from the church connection—the sacraments officiated by God's ordained ministers. The sacraments of baptism and the Lord's Supper occur with regularity at the church level. What do the sacraments actually do for us? I like how the Heidelberg Catechism defines sacraments:

> Sacraments are holy signs and seals for us to see. They were instituted by God so that by our use of them he might make us understand more clearly the promise of the gospel, and might put his seal on that promise. And it is God's gospel promise: to forgive our sins and give us eternal life by grace alone because of Christ's one sacrifice finished on the cross.

At a church service, the sacraments are something for us to see.

Every time we partake of Communion or someone is baptized, we are pointed toward God and his promises! To do this as a community is powerful encouragement for your familiar walk with God. You need to see this; your family needs to see this.

The Support of Prayer

The church connection puts you into contact with the "prayers of the saints." When godly people pray, it matters. Prayers spoken at the congregational worship service are important because God wants us to corporately pray for those in our church who have needs. Prayer at church also models for church members how to pray in their personal lives and with their families.

The book of James sees the work of the church as very connected to the ministry of prayer:

> Is any one of you sick? He should call the elders of the church to pray over him and anoint him with oil in the name of the Lord. And the prayer offered in faith will make the sick person well; the Lord will raise him up. If he has sinned, he will be forgiven. (James 5:14-15)

One of the testimonies to God's power I have heard numerous times is the value of a praying church. When someone experiences a loss or becomes ill, prayer from the corporate body is a powerful encouragement and support in the healing process.

The church also has the opportunity to help in the memorization of prayers such as the Lord's Prayer. This supports the talking-to-God efforts going on in people's homes.

The Support of Worship

There is something about corporate worship that greatly encourages a familiar walk with God. In worship, believers together humble themselves before God and glorify him as their

Lord. In the last twenty years, evangelical churches have drifted in their music selections to contemporary songs and have minimized the hymns. Many churches have "gone contemporary."

Though I enjoy contemporary songs, my wife and I felt convicted to introduce hymns into our own family and help other families also see hymns as important and loved. The first thing I did was to analyze why people loved contemporary songs and not the hymns. I thought it was because contemporary songs sounded like the songs people heard on the radio. But that didn't explain the many families I knew that still loved the hymns. The more time I spend around hymn singers, I noticed that to be familiar with a hymn is to love it. Families sing them over and over, and the hymns acquire layers of meaning. Familiarity is the critical piece!

Then I analyzed how song selection in a church further pushes people toward a specific worship-style preference. When I planted my first church, Community Life Church, we stressed the contemporary style. Under the excellent leadership of David Huizenga, we sang about fifty contemporary songs over and over again. These songs were done with unique Community Life Church flair. We grew to love contemporary songs. When we did occasionally sing a hymn, the hymn had to be either very familiar, like "Amazing Grace" or certain Christmas carols, or we had to spruce it up as a syncopated version that had rhythm. I lamented the loss of hymn culture.

How could hymns become loved again in Christian worship culture? The key is familiarity. We do not sing all six hundred hymns you find in a typical hymnbook. We sing about fifty hymns over and over. Each month we pick a hymn of the month to memorize. The first thing we do on Sundays is review the hymn of the month. And we even have added part singing to the mix. Our worship leader will ask the altos to stand and sing the alto part. The tenors stand, then the bass. Then the worship leader puts it all together. By the end of the month, we have learned a new hymn in beautiful harmony. Though our church sings contemporary songs as well and we enjoy them, now we also have the hymns. Even the very youngest like the hymns.

This hymn of the month is presented to the families of the church to practice at home. Christian Leaders has made a home-discipleship hymnbook with accompanying five-CD set. The CDs play all the hymns and their verses. They also play the four vocal parts for each hymn so families can practice part singing at home. (See Appendix A if you are interested in purchasing a set or developing a set for your church.)

A Key Concern:

One question potential church planters often ask me is, how does the church support individuals, couples, and families without making someone "feel" uncomfortable? On one level, protecting people's comfort may not be a realistic expectation. The church must challenge each of us to grow in a closer relationship with Christ. This challenge must include encouraging excellent doctrine and life practices; this challenge must include our spiritual habits and discipleship practices. This challenge, however, must be always measured with grace. Let's say you seek to be consistent in your home-discipleship practices but you fail. You want to be in a church that challenges you to try again. But you want to be in a church that acknowledges that it is difficult to maintain home-discipleship practices in our busy world. You want a church that reiterates that your relationship with God is won by grace, not by works or habits. Your familiar walk is not works-based. Therefore, home-discipleship churches do their best both to encourage excellent spiritual habits and to *graciously* encourage you to constantly face the difficulties in starting and maintaining a home-discipleship walk with God.

Personally, I haven't noticed a big trend toward people walking out the door, shaking their heads and thinking, "This is too much." In part, I think this is because we do not advertise our church as a place where you can enjoy the show and get a spiritual pick-me-up. The people who come to our church have usually already seen the home-discipleship practices modeled for them in the home of a neighbor or coworker. And what I hear most often is that people can't wait to get started. They have a spiritual dream, a drive to reach out and make a connection with the Almighty, a desire to be filled with the Spirit of God in a real and tangible way. After years of churches asking them to settle for less and just graze at a spiritual buffet, they are ecstatic to find a church that is going to challenge them to do more— to reach the high peak of the mountain of their spiritual dream.

Becoming spiritually disciplined and healthy is similar to developing good physical habits. Many find that they actually need to join the health club, paying real money to be supported to flex their muscles. Some even have to hire personal trainers to specially encourage them to do what they know they should do. The apostle Paul understood the problem when applied to our spiritual walk. He wrote:

> Everyone who competes in the games goes into strict training. They do it to get a crown that will not last; but we do it to get a crown that will last forever. Therefore I do not run like a man running aimlessly; I do not fight like a man beating the air. No, I beat my body and make it my slave so that after I have preached to others, I myself will not be disqualified for the prize. (1 Corinthians 9:25-27)

Willpower alone rarely works. Picking ourselves up by our bootstraps doesn't work. We need the accountability, support, structure, and personal investment that a church can provide in order to maintain a disciplined walk with God.

Chapter 10

Connection Six: The Kingdom Connection

I BEGAN this book speaking of the influence Rich DeVos had on my life as one of my mentors. Over the last ten years, I have attended many Orlando Magic basketball games as guests of the owners, Rich, and his wife, Helen. For the last ten years, I've had the opportunity to see the Magic win and lose with some of the premier players of the sport—Shaquille O'Neal, Penny Hardaway, Horace Grant, and Tracy McGrady. But what most impressed me was not the prowess of the individual players but the NBA organization and its role in supporting the game of basketball. To me this was a powerful illustration of the kingdom connection.

The game of basketball is played at many levels. I bought my son a little Nerf basketball hoop when he was five. We put a basketball hoop in our driveway when my son was seven. When others came over to our house, we often played basketball in some form or another. That's as far as the Reyenga family went in moving up the ladder as basketball players.

For many young people, the opportunity to advance in the game is abundant. There are school-sponsored teams, home-school group teams, city recreational leagues, the YMCA, office teams, and church-group teams. The fact is that basketball is a grassroots sports. It cannot be managed in all its parts by a single entity. The National Basketball Association is not able even to keep tabs on all the teams that have formed. It cannot control the quality or lack of quality of all the coaches who coach. It cannot make a church, school, city, or company start a basketball movement with a group of people; people play basketball because it is a great game. Yet there is a very important role the NBA plays in supporting, steering, and stirring the movement of basketball as a game.

The NBA organizes games where the very best players in the world compete. This is important because it gives every serious basketball player a place to compete at the highest level. Even if someone never makes it to the NBA, the dream of competing at the level inspires young people to practice and play the game at the level of their skill and aptitude. The NBA supports a fan movement, too. The game is great entertainment. I am amazed when I attend Magic games just how many fans really get into every aspect of the game. They could tell you very specific statistics from the careers of each player on the Magic. If there is a bad call by a referee, they will stand up and defend the honor of the home-team player. To many the game is a serious pastime, and winning and losing is very personal. The fans' role is very important because a stadium filled with throngs of cheering or booing fans elevates the importance of every game at the NBA level. The fans and sponsors also give the financial support to actually create this level of competition.

The NBA has other roles in developing the sport. There is a rules committee that reviews which rules govern the game at the major-league level. While other levels of basketball do not need to follow along, most will take any changes very seriously. Every grassroots movement, if it is sustainable, also needs guiding institutions like the NBA to update and contextualize the game in each generation. This was very true for the movement of basketball in our country. Can you imagine playing basketball the way it was founded in 1891?

Dr. James Naismith invented basketball in 1891. He was an instructor at a YMCA in Springfield, Massachusetts. Naismith wanted to come up with an indoor game that had a little rough play for the football and lacrosse players during the off-season. Teams consisted of nine players—a goalkeeper, home man, two guards (right and left), three centers (right center, left center, and center), and two wings (right and left).

Shortly after the game was invented, a league formed in 1898 called the National Basketball League. By the 1950s, the NBA was the premier league. Let me reveal just some of the important changes that had to be made at a level higher than local players of the game:

- 1894—Basketballs replace soccer balls.
- 1895—Backboards are introduced.
- 1908—The dribbler is allowed to shoot the ball.
- 1920—Players may reenter the game.
- 1932—The mid-court line is introduced to prevent teams from stalling.
- 1952—The free-shot line moves from 6 feet to 12 feet.
- 1954—The 24-second clock is introduced.
- 1964—The free-shot line extends to 16 feet.
- 1979—The NBA introduces a three-point line.

Can you imagine if there were not basketball "kingdom" connections to govern the game? How would you like to play the game of basketball with a soccer ball? Or what if players were not allowed to reenter a game? What if you were still making six-foot free throws? The fact is that "basketball kingdom" organizations like the NBA are very important for the game even at the grass roots.

The Importance of Kingdom Organizations

Believers have always benefited from various kingdom organizations that have supported grassroots Christianity. The grassroots movement was not very old when a kingdom council convened in Jerusalem to discuss some of the specific guidelines for Gentiles as the gospel spread throughout the land. This council met to support and steer the building of the new church. It is fascinating to read the account of this first assembly in Acts 15:1-30. There was a party of former Pharisees (Acts 15:5); the apostles and elders were represented (Acts 15:20); the great missionaries Paul and Barnabas attended. The council members gave speeches and made appeals. The apostle Peter delivered the keynote address, and the council went along with his appeal. By the end of the meeting, the council changed the specific rules and practices that govern new believers. Before the council, all converts to Christianity had to be circumcised as was customary for the Jewish religion. After the meeting, new non-Jewish converts did not have be circumcised. Here was the exact ruling:

> It seemed good to the Holy Spirit and to us not to burden you with anything beyond the following requirements: You are to abstain from food sacrificed to idols, from blood, from the meat of strangled animals and from sexual immorality. You will do well to avoid these things. Farewell. (Acts 15:28-29)

This meeting was the first official gathering of a council to address specific kingdom issues concerning grassroots Christianity. Kingdom councils have met over the centuries to support the grassroots movement of talking and listening repeatedly to God. Specific heresies were averted. Specific teachings about God were affirmed. Even the Bible books that we hold as "the Word of God" were first selected and then canonized. The kingdom connection has played an important role in the support and vivification of grassroots Christianity.

The universal church is all over the world. Today, there are kingdom organizations and denominations that support all sorts of ministry. These ministries support the sending of missionaries, church planting, disaster relief, third-world development, etc. There are kingdom ministries that support causes in the area of politics and the social-values debate.

The kingdom connection is also your connection to like-minded believers throughout the ages. You can establish and enrich this kingdom connection through reading books. The book *Pilgrim's Progress* has supported many believers' connections to God for generations. Today, hundreds of thousands of books written by Christians support a powerful kingdom connection for almost any area of life.

Christian colleges like Patrick Henry College are another example of a kingdom connection. These colleges are located in various parts of the world and are entrusted to educate Christian young people in a godly life and worldview. A great kingdom connection will support the success of some of the personal connections: For instance, Christian colleges have provided an effective place for courtship. Many believers have found their life partners while studying at these kingdom institutions.

A somewhat new kingdom connection is the advent of modern mass media, including TV, internet, film, magazines, and radio. Large numbers of people can access information quickly. Christians have sought to utilize these tools to proclaim the gospel effectively all over the world.

There are kingdom connections for your specific area of interest. As my family home schools, we connect to Christian home-schooling organizations such as the nonprofit Home School Legal Defense Association and publishing outfits that produce home-schooling materials.

The kingdom connection is that which is beyond our local

situation. Our walks with God have a kingdom connection that has spanned more than two thousand years and connects to others all over the world. This is a beautiful thing.

Possible Kingdom Pitfalls

We must be careful and discerning because we live in over-whelming times, when many potentially great causes or organizations beckon for our attention. Our kingdom connection may end up sidetracking us from a vital walk with God. A person could drift away from a home-discipleship familiar and intentional walk with God while focusing too much energy on a kingdom cause, person, or organization.

Kingdom Celebrities

I remember planting my first church back in the late 1980s. We were doing a telemarketing program to our geographic community. Many of the people I called had expressed open cynicism about Christianity because of the fall of recent television evangelists. At that time, two televangelists had fallen into sin's clutches: Jim Bakker and Jimmy Swaggart. Jim Bakker had built a massive theme park and television network with his wife, Tammy Faye Bakker. The only problem was that they were swindling the government and donors. Jimmy Swaggart was one of the most popular television evangelists; news came out that he was visiting prostitutes in hotel rooms.

I would invite people to church and they would ask me if I was looking to build a theme park. Some would tell me that they "actually got sucked into trusting Jimmy Swaggart and just look was happened." Passive watching of Christian television had somehow become a substitute for working out one's own salvation with fear and trembling. Many people were religiously following these ministries, and when these ministries fell, it was as if many fell with them.

What went wrong? The kingdom connection of television was for many people their only intentional discipleship connection. Many times these televangelists gave them the feeling of a close walk with God. These walks were usually weak and shallow, and when the celebrity disappeared, so did the people's connection to God.

The typical television preacher, even today, uses the same format that Jimmy Swaggart and Jim Bakker used in the 1980s. They present a very practical and inspiring message with the request or expectation that people will send in gifts to support this "important" ministry outreach. You never see a television evangelist make an appeal like: "Don't send us any money unless you are meeting with a like-minded body of believers that is supporting your home discipleship." Or how about: "Don't send us a dime unless you have family worship time."

Radio or Media Junkies

I have noticed over the years that many Christians have become religious-radio junkies. Their walk consists of listening to a preacher on the radio. They don't spend time with their family actually practicing home discipleship; they listen to Christian radio all day. I am not against Christian radio; I am against making the radio your walk with God while your family walks in a dry and weary land.

Many Christians get disgusted with the live music their church provides because their expectations for quality Christian music have risen by listening every day to artists performing hits recorded in a studio. Most worship choirs cannot compete to that level of excellence. People want at church what they hear on the radio, but a group of volunteers will never match what you hear on the radio or on a CD.

In the late 1990s, I came across a critique of the Jesus Film.

The Jesus Film is a cinematic depiction of the life of Christ that has been translated into scores of different languages. A missionary will find a way to go into the bush with a generator and show the Jesus Film. The actual showing of the film would be the first time many of the bush people have actually seen a motion picture. The technology is dazzling, the story is compelling, and at the end of the movie, many come forward and want to serve the God who gave his life to save humans from their sin. The sad fact is that, instead of giving people a talking-and-listening Christianity, we put in their spiritual DNA a media-mediated Christianity.

This is especially sad because in many of the third-world countries, the cities are rife with technology. Some cities do not have modern toilets or sewage treatment, but they have access to the internet and other media sources. Let's say a person sees the Jesus Film in the bush. He is impressed and makes a commitment to follow Jesus. Then he somehow finds his way into the city and he experiences films that have all the special effects. In retrospect, the Jesus Film wasn't all that impressive. Since his faith was not built on a talking-and-listening relationship with God, he does not grow beyond the shallow beginning.

I want to be clear about something: God uses all these means to spread the gospel. What I am emphasizing is that we shouldn't think our work is done as a church because we support a radio ministry or support the Jesus Film. The kingdom connection ought always to be encouraging the talking-and-listening success of the other connections—personal, marriage, family, fellowships, church, evangelism. If people show the Jesus Film, are they equally spending time pondering how to get a new convert to practice home discipleship?

Boundaries out of Balance
In many ways, we are in the heyday of kingdom-connection

ministries. Kingdom ministries do provide important ministry outreach, but things appear to be out of balance. I believe that we have to be very discerning as to what kingdom ministries to support. Here are some questions I would recommend asking:

- Is the ministry celebrity-focused? These types of ministry have inherent dangers: The celebrity could fall. The celebrity will eventually die. A direct connection to God in connection one (your personal life), two (your married life), and three (your family)—supported by connection four (your spiritually like-minded fellowship), five (your church), and six (kingdom connections that support your disciple-ship)—is the spiritual dynamic you need. You do not need to approach God on the coattails of someone famous.
- Does the ministry hurt historical orthodox Christianity? Anytime you come in contact with a ministry that puts practices or teachings into place that challenge the historical understanding of the teachings of the Bible, beware! Some denominations have left orthodox Christianity and have adopted teachings that actually reject the Bible as the Word of God.
- Does the kingdom ministry build up local churches? So many kingdom ministries are bypassing the local churches. The local church is where people know your name and can hold you accountable. The reason so many ministries bypass the local church is because there is less entanglement that way. A local church deals with real people in the complexities of their lives. A ministry can rally around one issue that everyone has in common, while not addressing the areas of disagreement and struggle. It's sad but true: Some people have given up on "real" local churches and have formed exclusive connections to kingdom ministries. When I worked at the Bible League,

we found that many donors did not go to a local church, but they gave money to send Bibles all over the globe. Even though the Bible League sent Bibles to be placed at local churches, many of the supporters did not attend such a church.

What About Denominations?

In the last twenty-five years, the strength of denominations has been declining while the presence of Christian ministries and nonprofits has been increasing. This is a troubling trend. By definition, denominations comprise local churches. The historical connection six would have to be denominations. This kingdom connection worked very well for generations. The reason it worked so well is that it existed to support the work of local churches. These denominations provided churches with seminaries for training ministers and Christian colleges for training in a biblical worldview. The denominational ministries came out of local church initiatives. Missionaries were sent. Disaster aid was given. Agencies were formed to do what one local church could not do alone. In theory, this kingdom connection effectively worked.

Why are some denominations decreasing in influence? In some cases, the leaders of the denominations have drifted away from very important grounding. Some denominations have become lax on historical doctrinal and lifestyle teachings. While some of these denominations seek to support churches that lead families and individuals, the nature of their support has drifted away from biblical Christianity.

Other denominations are decreasing in their influence because their own bureaucracies have stifled their ability to support grassroots Christianity. This happens in various ways:

Sometimes denominations adopt social agendas that center

on a valuable cause but do not necessarily support walking with God. The Methodist church started out so committed to home-discipleship practices that a person was required to attend a supportive fellowship group to get a ticket to go to the Sunday service. Eventually, the focus of their teaching shifted to the "social gospel," and the support for home discipleship was replaced by rallying around a social cause.

Sometimes denominations adopt certain cultural goals that do not reflect their core grassroots constituency. One common example of this is diversity goals. Let's say that the grassroots constituency is predominately white, from a European background. Then let us say that it is decided at kingdom level that a denomination should dramatically increase its cultural mix to include many different cultures and races. What happens is that a great amount of money, energy, and expertise is spent on creating a network of people that the denomination has no idea how to support; its infrastructure is set up to support a predominantly homogeneous people group. The original people end up struggling in their walks with God, because priorities have changed from supporting their walks to diversifying the people group.

Does that mean that denominations should not have diversity goals? No. But these goals have to balance with the needs of supporting that which is grassroots in a particular denomination. I've seen a very effective strategy within the Christian Reformed Church, traditionally a Dutch denomination. In the 1980s, Korean immigrants—who shared a CRC doctrinal and lifestyle Christianity—were welcomed by this predominately white European denomination to have a home in America. The Christian Reformed Church supported this grassroots people group by training Korean ministers at seminary, as well as other notable strategic and financial support. Today, there is a strong Korean presence in a predominantly white European denomination. In fact, there is even a classis (a classis is a large grouping of churches within the organizational structure) that consists solely of Korean churches.

The CRC had a goal of diversity, but that goal took into account the unique grassroots nature of people groups. The CRC did not try to create a Korean-European super service that somehow met the needs of both groups. Instead, these people groups found that they could support their grassroots expressions of Christianity when each of them gathered to support their unique cultures.

As America becomes more homogeneous, ethnic and racial barriers will cease to be central factors. More and more people will form new subcultures centered on like-mindedness in their values. Then the denominations will have to adjust to support these new grassroots people groups. This is already happening in many ways. I have seen in my own church (which has mostly home schoolers) a somewhat diverse ethnic makeup, yet we are homogeneous regarding our values and priorities.

Some may argue that this homogenous grassroots approach goes against the nature of the early church spreading to all nations. If I look at how the early church spread, I see distinctive people groups that knew how to support grassroots Christianity. The Jewish believers had certain practices distinct from the Gentile believers. Throughout history, the goal of most missionaries was to train indigenous leaders to lead others who spoke their language and lived the same kind of lives.

I look at it this way: To respect people is to respect their values and culture enough not to try to change them or make them be what they are not. Instead, respect is to support the walk of connection to God in the way that it is most practical for a given people group.

Let's say the denominational leadership feels called to reach out to a wide range of people groups beyond those it is already supporting. This must be done with real care and attention. Just getting people in the front door doesn't mean that you have created an environment in which they can thrive. You might actually be holding them back.

In my first church, we would have certain visitors who just did not fit our people group. One such person was a biker type. He hung around for a while, and we did everything we could to make him feel welcome. But I have to admit, I did not "understand" biker culture. When he would tell stories of his culture, they would amaze me "too much." When I would tell my stories, my culture was also too amazing for him. I did not know the nuances of his grassroots world, and he did not know my nuances.

This man left our church and went to a Foursquare church where the pastor had been a biker before he was saved. This man found his Christian people group. While he was at our church, in some unaware way we considered him a perpetual "new Christian." At this new church, the leaders there knew what this guy needed and what they should do. At our church, he would throw a few dollars in the collection plate. At this new church, he would tithe ten percent of his wages. At our church, he sensed that he would never really fit in. At this new church, he clicked on all cylinders.

On one level, we could be critical of our lack of cultural sensitivities. The church should be open to everyone. The biker should be as welcomed as the family man, right? Not necessarily. The journey of the biker and the family man are very different journeys. Each journey is to be respected as precious and whole when brought under the Lordship of Christ. The grassroots expressions of those journeys vary in such a profound way that our church cannot provide support for both types of journeys.

The point is that denominations are often caught up in figuring out how to expand their influence by casting a wide net, instead of focusing on deepening their influence among its current members. Denominations could regain their importance as a kingdom connection if, as the NBA supports a grassroots basketball culture, a denomination supports the grassroots practice of Christianity.

Kingdom Ministries

Any Christian ministry has a responsibility to support "church culture." The kingdom ministry role is to help churches do their local ministries even more effectively. Or, if a ministry aims directly at families, married couples, or individuals, the ministry must not knock these connections out of balance. For instance, if a ministry focuses on the family, that ministry should not teach or act in such a way that hurts the church connection. I have seen, for instance, a ministry that taught that patriarchy was so important that connection to a local church was optional. Another ministry was teaching that the church size for families should be no more than fifty to sixty people. Teachings such as these undermine local churches and the culture of paid ministers. The result is that a tent-making ministry becomes the only viable option for ministers. This is clearly not the way the early church was set up. The apostle Paul mentioned on various occasions that the workers deserve their wages.

Kingdom ministries should do whatever they can to ensure the building of Christian culture that supports home discipleship. Kingdom ministries need to have the following essential characteristics:

Grounded Leadership

A ministry must be grounded in Scripture. If a ministry is drifting, it will bring others along in that drift. Denominations, for instance, can provide excellent grounded doctrinal direction for their churches and do what one church alone cannot do. A study committee at the denominational level will include many trained and able theologians and ministers to figure out how to address an issue that faces churches. Usually this is very helpful and keeps the church from drifting away from what Scripture says. But if the leaders of a denomination themselves have drifted from the historical truth of Scripture, these leaders can cause many to stumble. It is important that the leaders of a denomination, or any kingdom ministry, are themselves accountable to the Scriptures and the confessional unity that has guided churches for centuries.

Great Commission

One church alone cannot begin to meet the demands of spreading the gospel in word and deed at home or in other lands. When large groups of churches and Christians get together, you can actually make a difference. If you scan the globe and research the missionary heritage of nearly every country, you would find that this was mainly the work of denominations and Christian ministries.

Broad Cultural Goals

Since the kingdom connection is larger than any one church, the kingdom ministry takes a bigger look at Christian culture than any one church can. Within an individual church, a move to encourage a multiethnic and multigenerational congregation affects a few hundred people, but within a denomination, it could set the course for thousands upon thousands. That means that a larger kingdom ministry will spend some resources to accomplish a goal that many individual churches would not have on their radar screens.

*   *   *

The Planting of a Culture

Kingdom ministries have the opportunity to plant a Christian culture in a way that a local church often cannot accomplish. I will share with you my dream for Christian Leaders, a Christian nonprofit that I founded in 2002 (www.homediscipleship.org). I sensed a call to plant home-discipleship culture all over the world. I am interested in seeing individuals, marriages, families, fellowships, and churches actually have a discipleship walk with God.

I believe one of the most important tasks in planting home-discipleship churches is creating a culture that encourages sustained and reproducible walks with God. As the NBA is to basketball, Christian Leaders and other similar ministries are trying to set the stage for developing grassroots playing of the game of Christianity. Christian Leaders supports the playing of the talking-and-listening game in the lives of the individual, marriage, and family. Lets call this backyard play.

At Christian Leaders, we want to form leagues. So we encourage you to form groups, fellowships, and new churches to play the game with more players. I know that when I play with others, I practice more on my own and I play the game in my backyard more. I believe that this type of church planting is exactly what the western world needs.

Conclusion

I CANNOT know, as you read this book, what level of familiarity you have with home-discipleship Christianity. Perhaps your church has been practicing home discipleship and you have been eager to really understand the concept in all its facets. Perhaps a friend has invited you to his or her home and you have seen a family practice home discipleship together. Perhaps you have been trying to lead others in home discipleship and you want the big picture. Whatever the case, I hope that prior to reading this book you had already been bitten by the home-discipleship bug. I hope that you have seen it in action. Reading about it is nothing like seeing the pride in your child's eyes as he or she recites a verse in front of the congregation. There is nothing like a warm handshake and a scrumptious meal in someone's home to make you understand that you are not alone in this process.

If you are reading this book without having visited a home-discipleship church or having seen home discipleship firsthand in the life of an ordinary family, then you are at a disadvantage. It is now time to stop reading about home discipleship and start living it, and it's very hard to do this on your own. Few of us are self-motivated enough to create a habit of Bible reading and prayer in our lives without the support and accountability of others who are trying to do the same thing; few of us are foolhardy enough to start a support group for talking and listening to God in the household with absolutely no prior success in personal Bible reading and prayer. Unfortunately, the seven connections are not a progression—you need all seven together, and they can be hard to launch all at once. Creating a culture is hard for a single individual or even a single family to do.

Two options remain to you: The first is to mentally check off the reasons why this would never work in your life. You can intellectually debate the concepts in this book and give yourself an excuse to close it and move on.

The second is to give it a try. Book a flight to the Midwest and visit one of our churches. Talk to people about how they got started in home discipleship. Send me a letter or an email and start a conversation with me. Order a home-discipleship journal and use it in your family. Have a family meeting, and talk and listen to God together. Fail at it. Learn from it. Talk to others about it. Ask people about their habits of connecting to God. To give you as much chance of succeeding as possible, I've included in Appendix E eight weeks' worth of direction for personal, marriage, and family devotions, as well as ways to kick-start your fellowship, church, kingdom, and world connections.

Ask others to read this book. Ask others to join you in eight weeks of talking and listening to God daily. Stir up the complacency a little in your church. (Of course, by all means possible, do not create dissension in your church or focus attention on yourself; be a blessing to the pastor and the church body.) Great things can happen from small beginnings. I know of dozens of families who started using the journal in their own homes and now have formed groups with other families nearby. It might not be easy, but then few things worth having are. You have to ask yourself what you truly desire in your life with God, and whether or not you can get there on your own.

If you do have a connection to others involved in home discipleship, the next step will be a little more simple: Make an effort to join that community. Come alongside like-minded friends in talking and listening to God together. Begin habits of reading the Bible and praying regularly. Start a family meeting in your home. Connect to God together with your spouse. Attend church with others involved in home discipleship. Sing together, memorize Scripture, eat together, listen to each other, and work together in your pursuit of deeper relationship with God. The culture is there; join it.

For some of you, you've been involved with home discipleship for a long time. You've helped others get started; you've led a small group of families in their goals of singing, learning to play instruments, getting the family together each night, reading through the Scriptures and discussing them each week. You know it works; you have been reading this book primarily to see how it works, or at least my vantage point on that question. You are searching for something more, that next step up. In that case, I invite you to join the Christian Leaders Institute (www.christianleadersinstitute.org) to be trained as a home-discipleship church planter.

Christian Leaders Institute offers ministry diplomas to people who are interested in learning how to plant and lead home-discipleship churches. The courses are offered primarily over the internet, with a few weeks a year of on-site learning. Instructors are experienced pastors and church planters, teaching courses that range from specifics on home discipleship, marriage, family, music, and evangelism to other pastoral concerns like hermeneutics, systematic theology, church history, and preaching. The biggest prerequisite for those interested in becoming leaders in home-discipleship Christianity is the belief that the most important church to plant is the church in one's own family. If you experience the call of God toward this ministry, your family will also be quite involved. While a new home-discipleship church often begins with organizational meetings explaining the concept of home-discipleship, the church really begins because a family that practices home discipleship is a powerful witness and discipleship agent to reach people who are not connected to God or a church. Please write me if you are interested in learning more about the institute.

I pray that this book will not end up on your shelf merely as a good read or a collection of interesting ideas. I hope that the idea of home discipleship will take root in you. This is not an idle hope. I have seen countless people who thought they could never begin a daily habit of Bible reading and prayer, succeed at it, and teach others to do the same. The movement is spreading. Now that you have been exposed to it, you have a choice to sit back and observe or to join the movement as a pioneer. Open the daily habits of your life to God himself and let him transform you. Give your family a unified purpose. Spread the message of Jesus Christ to those who live without hope. Whatever your first step on this journey might be, take it now.

Appendix A

The *Christian Leaders Home Discipleship Hymnbook* is designed to assist families and smaller groups with singing hymns. The list of hymns is included here if you want to get started trying a few right away. If you'd like to purchase a copy of the hymnbook, visit www.homediscipleship.org.

The hymbook is in a large format for easy reading and spiral bound for easy piano playing and contains suggested guitar chords for each hymn. An optional set of five CDs contains piano accompaniments for all the verses of each hymn. Following each hymn are individual tracks for the alto, tenor, and bass parts.

A Child of the King
A Mighty Fortress Is Our God
A Shelter in the Time of Storm
Abide with Me
All Hail the Power of Jesus' Name
Am I a Soldier of the Cross?
Amazing Grace
And Can It Be?
Angels, From the Realms of Glory
Angels We Have Heard on High
As with Gladness Men of Old
Be Thou My Vision

Beautiful Savior
Beneath the Cross of Jesus
Blessed Assurance
Breathe on Me, Breath of God
Christ the Lord Is Risen Today
Come, Thou Almighty King
Crown Him with Many Crowns
Doxology (Praise God, from Whom All Blessings Flow)
Faith Is the Victory
Faith of Our Fathers
Glorious Things of Thee Are Spoken
God Be with You Till We Meet Again
Hallelujah, Praise Jehovah (Psalm 148)
Hallelujah, What a Savior (Man of Sorrows! What a Name)
Hark, the Herald Angels Sing
Have Thine Own Way, Lord!
He Leadeth Me! O Blessed Thought!
Holy, Holy, Holy! Lord God Almighty
How Firm a Foundation
I Know Not Why God's Wondrous Grace
I Love to Tell the Story
I Need Thee Every Hour
It Is Well (When Peace Like a River)
Jehovah Is My Light
Jesus, Lover of My Soul
Jesus Loves Me
Jesus Saves (We Have Heard the Joyful Sound)
Jesus Shall Reign Wherever the Sun
Joy to the World!
Joyful, Joyful, We Adore Thee
Just As I Am
Lead On, O King Eternal
Lift High the Cross

Like a River Glorious
Lord Jesus, I Long to Be Perfectly Whole (Whiter Than Snow)
Low in the Grave He Lay
My Faith Has Found a Resting Place
My Jesus, I Love Thee
Nearer, Still Nearer
O Come, All Ye Faithful
O For a Thousand Tongues to Sing
O Worship the King, All Glorious Above
Onward, Christian Soldiers
Praise to the Lord, the Almighty
Rock of Ages, Cleft for Me
Silent Night, Holy Night
Stand Up, Stand Up for Jesus
Take My Life, and Let It Be
The Church's One Foundation
The Ends of All the Earth Shall Hear (Psalm 22)
The Solid Rock
This Is My Father's World
To God Be the Glory
We Gather Together
What a Fellowship, What a Joy Divine
What a Friend We Have in Jesus
When I Survey the Wondrous Cross
When Morning Gilds the Skies
Whole-hearted Thanksgiving to Thee I Will Bring (Psalm 9)

Appendix B

Two pages in the *Christian Leaders Family Journal* provide a week's worth of encouragement in doing home discipleship. On the right-hand page is a schedule coordinator, which has room to write each day's activities/prayer items, as well as reminders for daily devotions, song memory, and Scripture memory. On the left-hand page is the content for the weekly family meeting. The Scripture portion includes a reading, an exploration of the text, and questions for discussion. There is a space for family prayer needs, a checklist for each family member's spiritual habits, and a place to choose the week's hospitality contact.

To view a sample page of the journal or to order a copy, visit www.homediscipleship.org.

Appendix C

Choose a Bible-reading track based on the material you would like to cover or by how much time you can spend reading. The New Testament track and the 365 key chapters take five minutes a day; the whole-Bible track takes about fifteen each day.

365 Key Chapters:

Gen. 1	Gen. 50	Deut. 4	Ruth 1	1 Ki. 12	Neh. 1
Gen. 3	Ex. 1	Deut. 5	Ruth 2	1 Ki. 17	Neh. 2
Gen. 4	Ex. 2	Deut. 6	Ruth 3	1 Ki. 18	Neh. 4
Gen. 6	Ex. 3	Deut. 7	Ruth 4	1 Ki. 19	Neh. 5
Gen. 7	Ex. 4	Deut. 8	1 Sam. 1	2 Ki. 1	Neh. 6
Gen. 8	Ex. 5	Deut. 27	1 Sam. 2	2 Ki. 2	Neh. 8
Gen. 9	Ex. 6	Deut. 28	1 Sam. 3	2 Ki. 4	Neh. 9
Gen. 11	Ex. 7	Deut. 29	1 Sam. 8	2 Ki. 5	Esth. 1
Gen. 12	Ex. 8	Deut. 30	1 Sam. 9	2 Ki. 6	Esth. 2
Gen. 15	Ex. 9	Deut. 32	1 Sam. 10	2 Ki. 7	Esth. 3
Gen. 18	Ex. 10	Deut. 34	1 Sam. 15	2 Ki. 8	Esth. 4
Gen. 21	Ex. 11	Josh. 1	1 Sam. 16	2 Ki. 18	Esth. 5
Gen. 22	Ex. 12	Josh. 2	1 Sam. 17	2 Ki. 19	Esth. 6
Gen. 24	Ex. 13	Josh. 3	2 Sam. 5	2 Ki. 20	Esth. 7
Gen. 27	Ex. 14	Josh.4	2 Sam. 7	2 Ki. 25	Esth. 8
Gen. 28	Ex. 19	Josh. 6	2 Sam. 11	1 Chr. 17	Esth. 9
Gen. 37	Ex. 20	Josh. 23	2 Sam. 12	1 Chr. 29	Job 1
Gen. 39	Ex. 32	Josh. 24	1 Ki. 1	2 Chr. 34	Job 2
Gen. 40	Lev. 16	Jud. 2	1 Ki. 2	2 Chr. 35	Job 38
Gen. 41	Num. 13	Jud. 6	1 Ki. 3	Ezra 1	Job 39
Gen. 42	Num. 14	Jud. 7	1 Ki. 8	Ezra 3	Job 40
Gen. 43	Deut. 1	Jud. 14	1 Ki. 9	Ezra 4	Job 41
Gen. 44	Deut. 2	Jud. 15	1 Ki. 10	Ezra 5	Job 42
Gen. 45	Deut. 3	Jud. 16	1 Ki. 11	Ezra 6	Ps. 1

Ps. 19	Dan.3	Mark 6	Acts 22	Eph. 2	Heb. 4
Ps. 23	Dan. 4	Mark 8	Acts 23	Eph. 3	Heb. 8
Ps. 37	Dan. 5	Luke 1	Acts 24	Eph. 4	Heb. 9
Ps. 90	Dan. 6	Luke 2	Acts 25	Eph. 5	Heb. 11
Ps. 100	Dan. 9	Luke 4	Acts 26	Eph. 6	Heb. 12
Ps. 103	Hosea 4	Luke 7	Acts 27	Phil. 1	Heb. 13
Ps. 104	Hosea 14	Luke 15	Acts 28	Phil. 2	James 1
Ps. 105	Joel 2	Luke 16	Rom. 1	Phil. 3	James 2
Ps. 106	Amos 1	Luke 18	Rom. 2	Phil. 4	James 3
Ps. 107	Amos 2	Luke 19	Rom. 3	Col. 1	James 4
Ps. 145	Amos 9	Luke 20	Rom. 4	Col. 2	James 5
Prov. 1	Obad.	Luke 24	Rom. 5	Col. 3	1 Peter 1
Prov. 2	Jonah 1	John 1	Rom. 6	Col. 4	1 Peter 2
Prov. 3	Jonah 2	John 3	Rom. 7	1 Thes. 1	1 Peter 3
Prov. 4	Jonah 3	John 4	Rom. 8	1 Thes. 2	1 Peter 4
Prov. 5	Jonah 4	John 6	Rom. 12	1 Thes. 3	1 Peter 5
Prov. 6	Micah 5	John 8	Rom. 13	1 Thes. 4	2 Peter 1
Prov. 7	Micah 7	John 10	Rom. 14	1 Thes. 5	2 Peter 2
Prov. 8	Nahum 1	John 13	Rom. 15	2 Thes. 1	2 Peter 3
Prov. 9	Habb.3	John 14	1 Cor. 1	2 Thes. 2	1 John 1
Prov. 31	Zeph. 3	John 15	1 Cor. 2	2 Thes. 3	1 John 2
Ecc. 3	Haggai 1	John 16	1 Cor. 3	1 Tim. 1	1 John 3
Ecc. 12	Haggai 2	John 17	1 Cor. 6	1 Tim. 2	1 John 4
Song 1	Zech. 14	John 20	1 Cor. 7	1 Tim. 3	1 John 5
Is. 6	Mal. 3	John 21	1 Cor. 8	1 Tim. 4	2 John
Is. 40	Mal. 4	Acts 1	1 Cor. 9	1 Tim. 5	3 John
Is. 53	Matt. 5	Acts 2	1 Cor. 13	1 Tim. 6	Jude
Is. 55	Matt. 6	Acts 7	1 Cor. 15	2 Tim. 1	Rev. 1
Is. 61	Matt. 7	Acts 8	2 Cor. 1	2 Tim. 2	Rev. 2
Jer. 18	Matt. 13	Acts 9	2 Cor. 4	2 Tim. 3	Rev. 3
Jer. 19	Matt. 17	Acts 10	2 Cor. 5	2 Tim. 4	Rev. 4
Jer. 31	Matt. 21	Acts 13	2 Cor. 8	Titus 1	Rev. 5
Lam. 3	Matt. 24	Acts 15	2 Cor. 9	Titus 2	Rev. 19
Ezek. 1	Matt. 25	Acts 16	2 Cor. 12	Titus 3	Rev. 20
Ezek. 37	Matt. 26	Acts 17	Gal. 5	Philemon	Rev. 21
Dan. 1	Matt. 27	Acts 18	Gal. 6	Heb. 1	Rev. 22
Dan. 2	Matt. 28	Acts 21	Eph. 1	Heb. 2	

New Testament in One Year:

Matt. 1	Matt. 7	Matt. 12:1-21	Matt. 15:21-39	Matt. 20:1-16
Matt. 2	Matt. 8	Matt. 12:22-50	Matt. 16	Matt. 20:17-34
Matt. 3	Matt. 9:1-17	Matt. 13:1-32	Matt. 17	Matt. 21:1-22
Matt. 4	Matt. 9:18-38	Matt. 13:33-58	Matt. 18:1-20	Matt. 21:23-46
Matt. 5:1-26	Matt. 10:1-23	Matt. 14:1-21	Matt. 18:21-35	Matt. 22:1-22
Matt. 5:27-48	Matt. 10:24-42	Matt. 14:22-36	Matt. 19:1-15	Matt. 22:23-46
Matt. 6	Matt. 11	Matt. 15:1-20	Matt. 19:16-30	Matt. 23:1-22

Matt. 23:23-39	Luke 4:1-32	John 3:22-36	Acts 8:26-40	Rom. 14
Matt. 24:1-22	Luke 4:33-44	John 4:1-26	Acts 9:1-22	Rom. 15:1-13
Matt. 24:23-51	Luke 5:1-16	John 4:27-54	Acts 9:23-43	Rom. 15:14-33
Matt. 25:1-30	Luke 5:17-39	John 5:1-24	Acts 10:1-23	Rom. 16
Matt. 25:31-46	Luke 6:1-26	John 5:25-47	Acts 10:24-48	1 Co. 1
Matt. 26:1-19	Luke 6:27-49	John 6:1-21	Acts 11	1 Co. 2
Matt. 26:20-54	Luke 7:1-30	John 6:22-44	Acts 12	1 Co. 3
Matt. 26:55-75	Luke 7:31-50	John 6:45-71	Acts 13:1-23	1 Co. 4
Matt. 27:1-31	Luke 8:1-21	John 7:1-31	Acts 13:24-52	1 Co. 5
Matt. 27:32-66	Luke 8:22-56	John 7:32-53	Acts 14	1 Co. 6
Matt. 28:1-20	Luke 9:1-36	John 8:1-20	Acts 15:1-21	1 Co. 7:1-24
Mark 1:1-22	Luke 9:37-62	John 8:21-36	Acts 15:22-41	1 Co. 7:25-40
Mark 1:23-45	Luke 10:1-24	John 8:37-59	Acts 16:1-15	1 Co. 8
Mark 2	Luke 10:25-42	John 9:1-23	Acts 16:16-40	1 Co. 9
Mark 3:1-21	Luke 11:1-28	John 9:24-41	Acts 17:1-15	1 Co. 10-1-13
Mark 3:22-35	Luke 11:29-54	John 10:1-21	Acts 17:16-34	1 Co. 10:14-33
Mark 4:1-20	Luke 12:1-34	John 10:22-42	Acts 18	1 Co. 11:1-16
Mark 4:21-41	Luke 12:35-59	John 11:1-17	Acts 19:1-20	1 Co. 11:17-34
Mark 5:1-20	Luke 13:1-21	John 11:18-46	Acts 19:21-41	1 Co. 12
Mark 5:21-43	Luke 13:22-35	John 11:47-57	Acts 20:1-16	1 Co. 13
Mark 6:1-32	Luke 14:1-24	John 12:1-19	Acts 20:17-38	1 Co. 14:1-20
Mark 6:33-58	Luke 14:25-35	John 12:20-50	Acts 21:1-14	1 Co. 14:21-40
Mark 7:1-13	Luke 15:1-10	John 13:1-17	Acts 21:15-40	1 Co. 15:1-32
Mark 7:14-37	Luke 15:11-32	John 13:18-38	Acts 22	1 Co. 15:33-58
Mark 8:1-21	Luke 16:1-18	John 14	Acts 23:1-11	1 Co. 16
Mark 8:22-38	Luke 16:19-31	John 15	Acts 23:12-35	2 Co. 1
Mark 9:1-29	Luke 17:1-19	John 16:1-15	Acts 24	2 Co. 2-3
Mark 9:30-50	Luke 17:20-37	John 16:16-33	Acts 25	2 Co. 4
Mark 10:1-31	Luke 18:1-17	John 17	Acts 26	2 Co. 5
Mark 10:32-52	Luke 18:18-43	John 18:1-23	Acts 27:1-26	2 Co. 6
Mark 11:1-19	Luke 19:1-28	John 18:24-40	Acts 27:27-44	2 Co. 7
Mark 11:20-33	Luke 19:29-48	John 19:1-22	Acts 28:1-15	2 Co. 8
Mark 12:1-27	Luke 20:1-26	John 19:23-42	Acts 28:16-32	2 Co. 9
Mark 12:28-44	Luke 20:27-47	John 20	Rom. 1	2 Co. 10
Mark 13:1-13	Luke 21:1-19	John 21	Rom. 2	2 Co. 11:1-15
Mark 13:14-37	Luke 21:20-36	Acts 1	Rom. 3	2 Co. 11:16-33
Mark 14:1-25	Luke 22:1-30	Acts 2:1-13	Rom. 4	2 Co. 12
Mark 14:26-50	Luke 22:31-53	Acts 2:14-47	Rom. 5	2 Co. 13
Mark 14:51-72	Luke 22:54-71	Acts 3	Rom. 6	Gal. 1
Mark 15:1-26	Luke 23:1-26	Acts 4:1-22	Rom. 7	Gal. 2
Mark 15:27-47	Luke 23:27-38	Acts 4:23-37	Rom. 8:1-18	Gal. 3
Mark 16	Luke 23:39-56	Acts 5:1-16	Rom. 8:19-39	Gal. 4
Luke 1:1-23	Luke 24:1-35	Acts 5:17-42	Rom. 9	Gal. 5
Luke 1:24-56	Luke 24:36-53	Acts 6	Rom. 10	Gal. 6
Luke 1:57-80	John 1:1-28	Acts 7:1-19	Rom. 11:1-24	Eph. 1
Luke 2:1-24	John 1:29-51	Acts 7:20-43	Rom. 11:25-38	Eph. 2
Luke 2:25-52	John 2	Acts 7:44-60	Rom. 12	Eph. 3
Luke 3	John 3:1-21	Acts 8:1-25	Rom. 13	Eph. 4

Eph. 5	1 Tim. 1	Heb. 5	1 Peter 3	Rev. 5
Eph. 6	1 Tim. 2	Heb. 6	1 Peter 4	Rev. 6
Phil. 1	1 Tim. 3	Heb. 7	1 Peter 5	Rev. 7
Phil. 2	1 Tim. 4	Heb. 8	2 Peter 1	Rev. 8
Phil. 3	1 Tim. 5	Heb. 9	2 Peter 2	Rev. 9
Phil. 4	1 Tim. 6	Heb. 10:1-23	2 Peter 3	Rev. 10
Col. 1	2 Tim. 1	Heb. 10:24-39	1 John 1	Rev. 11
Col. 2	2 Tim. 2	Heb. 11:1-19	1 John 2	Rev. 12
Col. 3	2 Tim. 3	Heb. 11:20-40	1 John 3	Rev. 13
Col. 4	2 Tim. 4	Heb. 12	1 John 4	Rev. 14
1 Thes. 1	Titus 1	Heb. 13	1 John 5	Rev. 15
1 Thes. 2	Titus 2	James 1	2 John	Rev. 16
1 Thes. 3	Titus 3	James 2	3 John	Rev. 17
1 Thes. 4	Philemon	James 3	Jude	Rev. 18
1 Thes. 5	Heb. 1	James 4	Rev. 1	Rev. 19
2 Thes. 1	Heb. 2	James 5	Rev. 2	Rev. 20
2 Thes. 2	Heb. 3	1 Peter 1	Rev. 3	Rev. 21
2 Thes. 3	Heb. 4	1 Peter 2	Rev. 4	Rev. 22

Whole Bible in One Year:

Gen. 1-2	Ex. 38-40	Deut. 20-22	1 Sam. 21-24	1 Chr. 4-6
Gen. 3-5	Lev. 1-4	Deut. 23-25	1 Sam. 25-28	1 Chr. 7-9
Gen. 6-9	Lev. 5-7	Deut. 26-28	1 Sam. 29-31	1 Chr. 10-13
Gen. 10-11	Lev. 8-10	Deut. 29-31	2 Sam. 1-4	1 Chr. 14-16
Gen. 12-15	Lev. 11-13	Deut. 32-34	2 Sam. 5-8	1 Chr. 17-19
Gen. 16-19	Lev. 14-16	Josh. 1-3	2 Sam. 9-12	1 Chr. 20-23
Gen. 20-22	Lev. 17-19	Josh. 4-6	2 Sam. 13-15	1 Chr. 24-26
Gen. 23-26	Lev. 20-23	Josh. 7-9	2 Sam. 16-18	1 Chr. 27-29
Gen. 27-29	Lev. 24-27	Josh. 10-12	2 Sam. 19-21	2 Chr. 1-3
Gen. 30-32	Num. 1-3	Josh. 13-15	2 Sam. 22-24	2 Chr.4-6
Gen. 33-36	Num. 4-6	Josh. 16-18	1 Ki. 1-4	2 Chr. 7-9
Gen. 37-39	Num. 7-10	Josh. 19-21	1 Ki. 5-7	2 Chr. 10-13
Gen. 40-42	Num. 11-14	Josh. 22-24	1 Ki. 8-10	2 Chr. 14-16
Gen. 43-46	Num. 15-17	Jud. 1-4	1 Ki. 11-13	2 Chr. 17-19
Gen. 47-50	Num. 18-20	Jud. 5-8	1 Ki. 14-16	2 Chr. 20-22
Ex. 1-4	Num. 21-24	Jud. 9-12	1 Ki. 17-19	2 Chr. 23-25
Ex. 5-7	Num. 25-27	Jud. 13-15	1 Ki. 20-22	2 Chr. 26-29
Ex. 8-10	Num. 28-30	Jud. 16-18	2 Ki. 1-3	2 Chr. 30-32
Ex. 11-13	Num. 31-33	Jud. 19-21	2 Ki. 4-6	2 Chr. 33-36
Ex. 14-17	Num. 34-36	Ruth 1-4	2 Ki. 7-10	Ezra 1-4
Ex. 18-20	Deut. 1-3	1 Sam. 1-3	2 Ki. 11-14	Ezra 5-7
Ex. 21-24	Deut. 4-6	1 Sam. 4-7	2 Ki. 15-17	Ezra 8-10
Ex. 25-27	Deut. 7-9	1 Sam. 8-10	2 Ki. 18-20	Neh. 1-3
Ex. 28-31	Deut. 10-12	1 Sam. 11-13	2 Ki. 21-22	Neh. 4-6
Ex. 32-34	Deut. 13-16	1 Sam. 14-16	2 Ki. 23-25	Neh. 7-9
Ex. 35-37	Deut. 17-19	1 Sam. 17-20	1 Chr. 1-3	Neh. 10-13

Esth. 1-3	Ps. 100-102	Is. 52-54	Amos 4-6	Acts 19-21
Esth. 4-7	Ps. 103-105	Is. 55-57	Amos 7-9	Acts 22-24
Esth. 8-10	Ps. 106-108	Is. 58-60	Obad.-Jonah	Acts 25-26
Job 1-4	Ps. 109-111	Is. 61-63	Micah 1-4	Acts 27-28
Job 5-7	Ps. 112-114	Is. 64-66	Micah 5-7	Rom. 1-4
Job 8-10	Ps. 115-118	Jer. 1-3	Nah. 1-3	Rom. 5-8
Job 11-13	Ps. 119	Jer. 4-5	Hab. 1-3	Rom. 9-11
Job 14-17	Ps. 120-123	Jer. 6-8	Zeph. 1-3	Rom. 12-16
Job 18-20	Ps. 124-128	Jer. 9-12	Hag. 1-3	1 Cor. 1-4
Job 21-24	Ps. 129-132	Jer. 13-16	Zech. 1-2	1 Cor. 5-8
Job 25-27	Ps. 133-136	Jer. 17-20	Zech. 3-6	1 Cor. 9-12
Job 28-31	Ps. 137-139	Jer. 21-23	Zech. 7-10	1 Cor. 13-16
Job 32-34	Ps. 140-144	Jer. 24-26	Zech. 11-14	2 Cor. 1-3
Job 35-37	Ps. 145-147	Jer. 27-29	Mal. 1-4	2 Cor. 4-6
Job 38-42	Ps. 148-150	Jer. 30-32	Matt. 1-4	2 Cor. 7-9
Ps. 1-4	Prov. 1-3	Jer. 33-36	Matt. 5-7	2 Cor. 10-13
Ps. 5-8	Prov. 4-7	Jer. 37-39	Matt. 8-11	Gal. 1-3
Ps. 9-12	Prov. 8-11	Jer. 40-42	Matt. 12-15	Gal. 4-6
Ps. 13-15	Prov. 12-14	Jer. 43-46	Matt. 16-19	Eph. 1-3
Ps. 16-18	Prov. 15-18	Jer. 47-49	Matt. 20-22	Eph. 4-6
Ps. 19-21	Prov. 19-21	Jer. 50-52	Matt. 23-25	Phil. 1-4
Ps. 22-24	Prov. 22-24	Lam. 1-5	Matt. 26-28	Col. 1-4
Ps. 25-27	Prov. 25-28	Ezek. 1-3	Mark 1-3	1 Thes. 1-5
Ps. 28-30	Prov. 29-31	Ezek. 4-7	Mark 4-6	2 Thes. 1-3
Ps. 31-33	Eccl. 1-3	Ezek. 8-11	Mark 7-10	1 Tim. 1-3
Ps. 34-36	Eccl. 4-6	Ezek. 12-14	Mark 11-13	1 Tim. 4-6
Ps. 37-39	Eccl. 7-9	Ezek. 15-18	Mark 14-16	2 Tim. 1-4
Ps. 40-42	Eccl. 10-12	Ezek. 19-21	Luke 1-3	Titus 1-3
Ps. 43-45	Song 1-4	Ezek. 22-24	Luke 4-6	Philemon
Ps. 46-48	Song 5-8	Ezek. 25-27	Luke 7-9	Heb. 1-4
Ps. 49-51	Is. 1-3	Ezek. 28-30	Luke 10-13	Heb. 5-7
Ps. 52-54	Is. 4-6	Ezek. 31-33	Luke 14-17	Heb. 8-10
Ps. 55-57	Is. 7-9	Ezek. 34-36	Luke 18-21	Heb. 11-13
Ps. 58-60	Is. 10-12	Ezek. 37-39	Luke 22-24	James 1-2
Ps. 61-63	Is. 13-15	Ezek. 40-42	John 1-3	James 3-5
Ps. 64-66	Is. 16-18	Ezek. 43-45	John 4-6	1 Peter 1-2
Ps. 67-69	Is. 19-21	Ezek. 46-48	John 7-10	1 Peter 3-5
Ps. 70-72	Is. 22-24	Dan. 1-3	John 11-13	2 Peter 1-3
Ps. 73-75	Is. 25-27	Dan. 4-6	John 14-17	1 John 1-2
Ps. 76-78	Is. 28-30	Dan. 7-9	John 18-21	1 John 3-5
Ps. 79-81	Is. 31-33	Dan. 10-12	Acts 1-2	2 Jn.-Jude
Ps. 82-84	Is. 34-36	Hosea 1-4	Acts 3-5	Rev. 1-3
Ps. 85-87	Is. 37-39	Hosea 5-7	Acts 6-9	Rev. 4-8
Ps. 88-90	Is. 40-42	Hosea 8-10	Acts 10-12	Rev. 9-12
Ps. 91-93	Is. 43-45	Hosea 11-14	Acts 13-14	Rev. 13-15
Ps. 94-96	Is. 46-48	Joel 1-3	Acts 15-16	Rev. 16-18
Ps. 97-99	Is. 49-51	Amos 1-3	Acts 17-18	Rev. 19-22

Appendix D

Timeless Scripture-memorization suggestions:

Genesis 1:27-31 — Cultural mandate
Genesis 2:19-25 — The creation of marriage
Exodus 20:1-17 — The Ten Commandments
Deuteronomy 6:1-9 — The pattern of walking with God
Joshua 24:14-15 — Household faith commitment
Ruth 1:16-17 — Godly loyalty
1 Chronicles 4:10 — The prayer of Jabez
Job 19:25-27 — Resurrection hope
Psalm 1 — Contrast life's two roads
Psalm 8 — God, the all-powerful Creator
Psalm 16 — Benefits and joys of a life in God
Psalm 23 — A "must memorize"
Psalm 24 — God, the glorious King
Psalm 27 — God is our help and our hope-giver
Psalm 46 — God is our fortress
Psalm 51 — A power prayer of confession
Psalm 90 — Seize the day
Psalm 91 — God's protection
Psalm 100 — Joyfully entering God's presence
Psalm 103 — God's great love for us
Psalm 117 — Shortest chapter of the Bible
Psalm 119:9-16 — The pure way
Psalm 119:145-152 — An urgent prayer
Psalm 121 — Dependence on God
Psalm 139 — God's knowledge of us
Psalm 150 — A hymn of rejoicing

Proverbs 3:5-6 — Trusting in the Lord
Proverbs 22:6 — Training in the Lord
Proverbs 31:10-31 — The noble woman
Ecclesiastes 3:1-14 — A time for everything
Ecclesiastes 12:1-14 — The end of the matter
Song of Songs 8:6-7 — Love as strong as death
Isaiah 40:28-31 — God makes us soar
Isaiah 53 — The suffering Servant
Isaiah 55:1-12 — God's invitation
Jeremiah 29:11-13 — God's plan to prosper
Ezekiel 36:25-27 — A new heart
Lamentations 3:21-23 — Great is God's faithfulness
Daniel 12:2-3, 13 — A great finish
Micah 6:8 — God's requirement
Zephaniah 3:17 — God's singing over a believer
Malachi 3:10 — The joy of tithing
Matthew 5:3-10 — The Beatitudes
Matthew 6:25-33 — Seeking the Kingdom first
Matthew 11:28-30 — Rest for the weary
Matthew 27:45-54 — The Crucifixion of Jesus
Matthew 28:16-20 — The Great Commission
Luke 2:1-18 — The birth of Jesus
Luke 12:8-11 — Acknowledging Christ
John 1:1-5, 14 — God became a human in Christ
John 3:16 — A "must memorize"
John 10:14-18 — Jesus, the Good Shepherd
John 14:1-6 — Jesus, the way to heaven
John 17:1-5 — Jesus shares his purpose
John 20:1-8 — The resurrection of Jesus
John 20:24-30 — Jesus appears to Thomas
Acts 1:8 — God's witnesses
Acts 2:38-39 — Gospel invitation
Acts 4:12 — The only name that saves
Romans 3:21-26 — Forgiveness through Christ
Romans 5:6-8 — God's demonstrated love
Romans 8:28-39 — More than conquerors in Christ
Romans 12:9-21 — Instructions for living
1 Corinthians 13 — The "love" passage
2 Corinthians 4:7-17 — Eyes on the eternal

2 Corinthians 5:6-10 — By faith not sight
2 Corinthians 5:16-21 — Ministry of reconciliation
Galatians 3:26-29 — In Christ, children of God
Galatians 5:22-25 — The fruit of the Spirit
Ephesians 3:14-20 — A prayer for power
Ephesians 5:15-21 — A godly lifestyle
Ephesians 5:22-33 — Husband and wife
Ephesians 6:1-3 — Children
Ephesians 6:10-18 — The armor of God
Philippians 1:20-21 — Living or dying in Christ
Philippians 2:1-11 — A believer's attitude
Philippians 4:4-9 — Rejoice in the Lord
Colossians 1:15-20 — Christ is supreme
Colossians 3: 1-17 — How Christians should live
1 Thessalonians 4:13-18 — The second coming of Jesus
1 Thessalonians 5:15-24 — Key wisdom
1 Timothy 1:15-17 — A trustworthy saying
1 Timothy 6:6-10 — Contentment
2 Timothy 1:12-14 — Guarding the good deposit
2 Timothy 4:6-8 — Longing for Christ
Titus 2:11-14 — Saying yes to God's will
Hebrews 4:12 — The Word of God is like a sword
Hebrews 10:32-29 — A great contest
Hebrews 11 — The heroes of faith
Hebrews 12:1-3 — Eyes on Jesus
James 1:22-27 — Doing God's will
James 3:3-12 — Taming the tongue
James 4:13-16 — The Lord willing
1 Peter 1:3-9 — The living hope
1 Peter 4:7-11 — Living for God
2 Peter 1:3-11 — The unfolding of the Spirit's work
1 John 1:5-10 — Walking in the light
1 John 2:15-17 — How to understand sinful culture
1 John 3:16-20 — Love in action
Revelation 22:1-5 — The new heaven and earth

Appendix E

For the next eight weeks, you will attempt to spend at least 25 minutes each day doing home discipleship: 5 minutes of personal devotions, 5 minutes of marriage devotions, and 15 minutes of talking and listening to God as a family. At the start of each week, you will focus some attention on your church connection. Every four weeks, give attention to your fellowship connection and kingdom connection as well. At the end of all eight weeks, zero in on your world connection and find a family that you can introduce to walking with God on a regular basis.

If you like, buy a blank notebook and jot down your thoughts on the readings and your prayers each day. This will also help you to remember when a week or four weeks has passed and you can spend some time thinking about all of the connections.

Connection One—A personal walk with God
Purpose: To strengthen your intentional walk with God.
Agenda: Spend time alone with God for at least five minutes each day, talking and listening to him by reading a passage from the Bible and praying.
Reading suggestions: Luke 1-24, Acts 1-28, Philippians 1-4 (one chapter each day)

*   *   *

Connection Two—A marriage walk with God

Purpose: To strengthen your intentional walk with your spouse by walking with God together.

Agenda: Spend time together with God for at least five minutes each day, talking to God by praying aloud together and listening to him by reading passages of the Bible. (Note: An added practice that will enrich your marriage is to read Christian material that encourages your marriage walk.)

Reading suggestions for 56 days: Genesis 18:1-15, 29:14-30, 39; Exodus 2:11-14, 4:18-29, 18; Deuteronomy 6; Joshua 6:1-15; Judges 16; Ruth 1, 2, 3, 4; 1 Samuel 1; 2 Samuel 11, 12; Psalm 1, 3, 16, 24, 25, 32, 46, 51, 62, 71, 103; Proverbs 18, 30; Ecclesiastes 7; Song of Songs 1, 2, 3, 4, 5, 6, 7, 8; Matthew 6:25-34; Romans 14; 1 Corinthians 7, 13; 2 Corinthians 5:11-21; Galatians 5; Ephesians 5; Philippians 4; Colossians 3; 1 Thessalonians 4:1-12; 1 Timothy 2, Titus 2, Hebrews 13, James 4, 1 Peter 3, 1 John 4, Revelation 22.

Connection Three—The family connection to God

Purpose: To help your family grow close through a committed walk with God, and to raise future Christian leaders.

Agenda: Gather as a family for at least fifteen minutes to read a chapter from the Bible (suggestions focused on home discipleship can be found below), memorize a verse or passage (see appendix D), sing together (see appendix A or visit www.home-discipleship.org to download the hymn of the month), and pray together as a family.

Reading suggestions for 56 days: Genesis 2, 3, 4, 6; Exodus 1, 2, 3, 20; Deuteronomy 6; Joshua 1; 1 Samuel 1, 4, 17; 2 Samuel 2; 2 Kings 22; Psalm 23, 24, 27, 90, 91, 139; Ecclesiastes 3; Proverbs 31; Daniel 6; Matthew 27, 28; Luke 2; John 14, 17, 19, 20, 21; Acts 1, 7, 9; Romans 8; 1 Corinthians 13; 2 Corinthians 4; Galatians 5; Ephesians 5, 6; Philippians 2,

3; Colossians 3; 1 Thessalonians 1; 1 Timothy 3; 2 Timothy 1, 4; Hebrews 11, 12; James 3; 1 Peter 1; 2 Peter 1; 1 John 1; 3 John; Revelation 21.

Connection Four—Like-minded fellowship

Purpose: Through exercising hospitality, to find others who are of a like mind to start or support a home-discipleship practice.

Agenda: At least twice during the eight weeks, invite over another family to have dinner and share home-discipleship practices together.

—Potluck dinner together

—Family Bible reading from your schedule for the day

—Families sharing what they are memorizing

—Singing the hymn of the month together

—Prayer

Connection Five—The church connection

Purpose: To talk and listen to God together within the context of a church community on Sunday mornings through song, the sermon, the sacraments, and fellowship.

Agenda: Attend church each week during the eight weeks, and at least once, invite another family to visit your church.

Connection Six—The kingdom connection

Purpose: To build your family's relationship with other Christians throughout the world.

Agenda: At least twice during the eight weeks, complete a suggestion from the list below or create your own way of connecting to kingdom organizations or people.

—Write a letter to missionaries

—Attend a denominational conference or ecumenical event

—Volunteer for a service project for a Christian organization

—Read from a historical Christian book out loud as a family
—Pray for Christians who are persecuted in other countries

Connection Seven—Home-discipleship evangelism

Purpose: Through the ministry of hospitality, to help people get started in a walk with God.

Agenda: At the end of the eight weeks, have over for dinner a family that needs to be introduced to walking with God. Share home-discipleship practices with them.

Acknowledgements

SO MANY people contributed to and supported the completion of this book. Since the mid-'80s, I have worked with a myriad of Christian leaders who helped shape the ideas and concepts.

I want to thank my wife, Pamela, and my children, Henry John, and his wife, Melissa, Brianna, Christina, Ann, and Abigail for their willingness to follow a home-discipleship pattern and lifestyle in our home. The members of my family made many contributions to this project.

I want to recognize Rich DeVos for his contribution to understanding reproducible forms of evangelism and discipleship. Rich is the type of encourager who makes ordinary people dream great dreams and then actually succeed.

I acknowledge the intellectual contribution that Steve Elzinga has made in shaping how I think about leadership. Many of the ideas in this book were formulated in years of dialogue since 1990. The actual seven-connection structure around which this book is organized comes from Steve's brilliant mind.

I want to thank Mike Farris and many others for challenging me to write this book. After spending three days with Michael and Vicky Farris, my wife and I were challenged to take that next step in kingdom faithfulness.

The people at Family of Faith Church have made a huge contribution. Rev. David Feddes, the cofounding pastor, and the elders, leaders, and participants in home discipleship have contributed greatly to this book in various profound ways.

Special thanks to Steve Lansingh and Amanda Caldwell for their great work in revisions, editing, and layout.

Special thanks to Rinck Heule for his printing expertise and contribution.

Special thanks to Lorene Franklin for her many contributions. She brings excellence to whatever she does.

I want to thank Carl and Paula Heule for their support in printing this project for distribution.

Finally, most importantly, I want to thank God for his grace and presence in our Lord Jesus Christ. God has given our family the opportunity to proclaim the Gospel. We are having such joy in this calling!

About the Author

Henry Reyenga Jr. is senior pastor at Family of Faith Church in Monee, Illinois. Henry and his wife, Pam, have led their five children in daily habits of Bible reading, prayer, Scripture memorization, and family worship—home discipleship—from the start, and Henry has been involved with four church plants since graduating from Calvin Theological Seminary in 1987.  These pursuits dovetailed in 2000 with the formation of a home-discipleship church, which has sponateously spread into a growing network of churches. Henry is the founder of Christian Leaders, a ministry supporting home discipleship as a movement, and is president of the Christian Leaders Institute, which trains church planters in the practice of home discipleship. Henry can be reached at leaders@homediscipleship.org.